Changing Attitudes and Behavior

Other Titles of Interest by
Rowman & Littlefield Education

Teaching Students to Work Harder and Enjoy It:
Practice Makes Permanent
by John Jensen

Effective Classroom Turnaround: Practice Makes Permanent
by John Jensen

Discipline without Anger: A New Style of Classroom Management
by Doug Campbell

The Classroom Manager:
Procedures and Practices to Improve Instruction
by Suzanne G. Houff

Crisis Prevention and Intervention in the Classroom:
What Teachers Should Know,
second edition by Victoria B. Damiani

Learning From Behavior:
How to Understand and Help 'Challenging' Children in School
by James E. Levine

Diagnosis and Remediation Practices for
Troubled School Children
by Harold F. Burks

Banishing Bullying Behavior:
Transforming the Culture of Peer Abuse,
second edition by SuEllen Fried and Blanche Sosland

Books, Blackboards, and Bullets:
School Shootings and Violence in America
by Marcel Lebrun

Changing Attitudes and Behavior

Practice Makes Permanent

John Jensen

ROWMAN & LITTLEFIELD EDUCATION
A division of
ROWMAN & LITTLEFIELD PUBLISHERS, INC.
Lanham • New York • Toronto • Plymouth, UK

MT

Published by Rowman & Littlefield Education
A division of Rowman & Littlefield Publishers, Inc.
A wholly owned subsidiary of The Rowman & Littlefield Publishing Group, Inc.
4501 Forbes Boulevard, Suite 200, Lanham, Maryland 20706
www.rowman.com

10 Thornbury Road, Plymouth PL6 7PP, United Kingdom

British Library Cataloguing in Publication Information Available

Library of Congress Cataloging-in-Publication Data

Jensen, John, 1935- author.
Changing attitudes and behavior : practice makes permanent / John Jensen.
pages cm
Includes bibliographical references.
ISBN 978-1-61048-803-7 (cloth : alk. paper) -- ISBN 978-1-61048-804-4 (pbk. : alk. paper) -- ISBN 978-1-61048-805-1 (electronic) (print)
1. Teaching--Methodology. 2. Learning, Psychology of. 3. Motivation in education. I. Title.
LB1025.3.J465 2012
371.102--dc23
2012013617

™
The paper used in this publication meets the minimum requirements of American National Standard for Information Sciences Permanence of Paper for Printed Library Materials, ANSI/NISO Z39.48-1992.

Printed in the United States of America

1/29/13

Contents

Preface   vii

1   Pursue Continuous Conscious Mastery: *A goal that unifies methods*   1

2   Sequence Learning Activities Optimally: *Arrange a reliable learning system*   7

3   Arrange for Good Feelings: *Why bring balance to students' feelings*   19

4   Practice Good Feelings: *Methods for generating good feelings*   35

5   Practice with the Imagination: *Drawing most benefit from imagination*   61

6   Practice Sustaining Attention: *Hold students' attention steadily*   69

7   Draw on Social Roots: *Students cue each other's learning*   77

8   Alter Thinking to Gain Order: *Change behavior by changing thinking*   89

9   Turn Around a Dysfunctional Class: *Bring multiple influences to bear*   121

10   Hone Your Viewpoint: *Key zones for teacher intent*   137

11   Know What You Are Doing: *Grasp the difficulties of change*   145

12   Hold Out for the Plus Element: *Even good education is not enough*   161

Preface

This book is a companion to two others: *Teaching Students to Work Harder and Enjoy It: Practice Makes Permanent* and *Effective Classroom Turnaround: Practice Makes Permanent.*

While each stands alone as a guide for better classroom results, each has an emphasis. The first above focuses on principles behind academic progress; the second, on succinct descriptions of key methods for both academics and attitude. This book examines issues of attitude and behavior to help make teacher interventions easy and effective. Core principles reappear from different angles.

A challenge in writing this series has been giving due emphasis to subtle forces at work. One continually asks, "How much of this under what conditions?" We always work within ongoing perceptions. Are students ready for this right now? Can elusive influences sabotage what we attempt? What do we foresee from the conditions we arrange? We wrestle here with the values and emotions of students and teachers that are most likely to undermine our efforts if misjudged.

As a common starting point, I assume that we first understand human nature accurately and then attempt to optimize its actions through conditions we supply. The unifying thread of this series is a particular condition—the use of practice—an underused activity that I believe could transform education if employed properly. If somehow I have drawn unwarranted conclusions from experience and research, I urge readers to pass on their ideas to me. The many facets of education suggest that we will always have more to learn about it.

A school staff becomes a team, one might say, as individuals adopt a common plan and support each other in carrying it out. We need an idea that appeals to everyone and then care enough about it to implement it together. The first chapter offers a unifying goal, continuous conscious mastery. Next we combine essential steps into a sequence that reliably achieves it, drawing on key ideas from the other two books of the series. In the remaining chapters, we treat the affective dimension in more detail.

John Jensen
November 2011

ONE

Pursue Continuous Conscious Mastery

A goal that unifies methods

THE SIMPLICITY OF IT

"Practice makes perfect" describes a facet of human functioning. It relates to all learning but has not been applied everywhere needed. A familiar problem illustrates: learning children's names.

You grasp a face, grasp a name, and put the two together, but your task is not done. Unless you return to the knowledge soon, you start over later, seizing on data bits (appearance, race, gender, height, sociability) to confirm the link—face with name. In a few days, you have recalled it repeatedly. It becomes so familiar and correct that you wonder how you could ever *not* have known it.

That picture is a fair model of what we do in learning anything deeply. Before we can practice, we must at least get the answer right. But from there to the point of automaticity, the continuum of progress *is solely from practice.*

One could plot a distribution of the number of repetitions needed to reach the confident/automatic use of a child's name. Seldom does it occur on one trial—remembering permanently everything about this child by noting the data field once. Repeating it until confident of it is what we call practice—repetition to develop a skill.

A realization with the potential to transform education is that everything we want to teach lies on this continuum. Each bit requires a varying number of repetitions for ultimate mastery, which tells us exactly what to do with every new idea we teach: 1) provide them an accurate take on it, and then 2) they repeat it the number of times required to assimilate it while varying the manner as needed. If a child does not get it yet, we make sure his initial grasp of it is correct and then place him on a track of practice leading to its assimilation. The skill evolves as mastery of parts enables faster thought processes.

To apply this simple idea amid the forms of education, we have much more to say, but throughout, practice continues to "make perfect" and even permanent.

A MODEL OF LEARNING

We can begin with what we know we do not want: familiarized, superficial, forgettable learning; inchoate, ill-formed, unexpressed knowledge that passes minimal tests; little expression of learning, leaving students passive and quiet with their knowledge; expecting mastery without sustained effort; piecemeal, overspecific, minimum curricular goals; blaming students for not learning under conditions hostile to their needs.

We do not want vague grades and evaluations that provide no information about what students actually know—ignoring students' social/emotional skills and happiness, correcting behavior without changing thinking, enforcing rules without understanding what occurs inside students.

Instead we pursue learning consciously *retained*. While acknowledging that students absorb random and temporary ideas, we select what we want them to learn permanently and design instruction to achieve that. We credit them with valid learning when students can *explain* a chunk of knowledge without help and maintain it at that level. We recognize that to integrate new knowledge with their thinking and values, students must express and re-express it, often in their own words.

Achieving mastery depends on time spent in incremental, hourly *practice* in which students organize and explain to partners what they understand and produce it without help in varied forms over an extended period. Our aim extends far beyond a single set of questions. We want students to *learn everything possible*, an open-ended goal, explaining entire courses beginning to end.

In pursuing these aims, we draw on their innate motivation to meet their needs. They change instantly when their learning activity aligns with their *intrinsic drives*. They are more motivated when they can *score* the results of their effort objectively, accurately, and reliably, and deserve a cumulative record of everything they learn. Their *affective* self-management is essential to learning and can be developed through discussion, feedback, appreciation, goal setting, progress rating, agreement making, and explanation.

Their learning becomes more significant as they can demonstrate it. They study harder when they expect to *perform* it before applauding peers and parents. We obtain their discipline and cooperation best by altering their *thinking*. Teachers need to respect students and apply small, fair, and foreseeable consequences for cooperation and misbehavior. We teach so that students are *happy*—and happy at learning.

In threading our way through classroom conditions while implementing the picture above, it helps to have an idea that, with one phase completed, points us unerringly to the next. We note this linkage constantly with content—learning one thing and building on it to learn another—but it applies also to methods. We want to know what activity builds on a prior.

Assume that you teach fractions and introduce numerator and denominator. You explain them, write them on the board, and ask everyone to copy them. You do not expect that to be the last time you deal with those terms. They have barely arrived on the front porch of students' minds, so you may give examples, call on students, and point to one number after another, asking them to label each correctly or write out formal definitions everyone copies. And then . . . ? What takes this learning securely onward?

CONTINUOUS CONSCIOUS MASTERY

A unifying, guiding goal enabling you to select one activity over another is *continuous conscious mastery*. Moving toward it, students first grasp knowledge *accurately* (like the correct take on a name) and then *deeply* (by practicing it). As we present a new section, the initial impression we get across may not be enough. They need not just an impression but also a perfect one. Looking at a child's printed name, you wonder, "Is that child 'Arian' or 'Anian'?" We have to get it straight before we can deepen it.

While it may seem an obvious point, the clarity of our very first answer is a huge systemic problem. Parents and subsequent teachers may be asked to help a child with an assignment *for which prior class time provided them no understanding whatever*. They did not get what the teacher said, lost their way in the book, or failed to grasp the question.

We refrain from blaming students or their parents for the deficit. A value we expect from our system is that differences in student ability or preparation do not change our mandate. We can even assume that we have a heterogeneous class. What was a K–8 classroom in the early days anyway? It meant that everyone took the step *next for them*. But for a spectrum of ability among students enrolled in one subject, if you permit one not to understand what others do and are moving on from, hour by hour talk passes around him. Continually he mumbles, "I don't get it," and eventually concludes that something is wrong with him because he is expected to get it.

If you and your system do not acknowledge your obligation to catch up this slower runner to the rest, you declare some children disposable. If instead a child's life is important, you utilize your resources in a manner enabling him to catch up. "Sounds good in principle," you murmur, "but if class enrollment is set and I have a big class to manage, what do I do?"

Return to basic values and purposes. *Engage the entire class in the success of each.* While all the facets of a learning community contribute, a specific tack is to pair them up, assigning the most helpful to those who need help most. Treat every pair as a team in all ways you can but especially in the initial step of getting each new answer perfect and complete in everyone's head. With fractions, the pairs ask each other to define numerator and denominator, give examples, compare what they hear to the correct written answer, and raise their hand when they both know it. Once they have a perfect answer, we can proceed toward continuous conscious mastery.

Their first try at the answer is only temporary mastery not yet continuous and conscious. "Continuous" means they can express it reliably any time asked. They still have it at 8 a.m. the next morning. Once gained it is never lost, so that when the point comes up later, they can respond correctly. "Conscious" contrasts here with latent. It is at their disposal. They can look inside their mind and there it is without prompting or help, can call it up without being asked the question, can *initiate* talking about it. If they are then able to explain it to someone else without help, we call that mastery. With continuous conscious mastery, your goal for that piece of knowledge is complete.

BREADTH AND DEPTH

From there, mastery expands along two dimensions. One is adding *more* knowledge, having more to say. A second independent measure is *depth*. One may have much of the first and little of the second: "His learning was like the Powder River—a mile wide and an inch deep."

Depth can be plotted objectively by counting up *the increasing number of days one can still produce a perfect answer since last looking at the material.* A student brimming with knowledge from a weekend of cramming we credit with breadth but, lifting the covers on his knowledge, minimal depth. A week later he would flunk.

These measures express our instructional aim: knowledge broad and deep maintained in continuous, conscious mastery. Next we look at how to obtain it.

SUMMARY

1. The simplicity of practice lies in the repetition and development of a correct model.
2. From an initial correct answer for any knowledge, further progress with it lies on the continuum of practice.
3. We do not want vague, piecemeal, poorly assimilated knowledge.
4. We want knowledge retained, explained, practiced, performed, aligned with intrinsic drives, scored; for students to learn everything possible, their feelings and attitudes addressed, and for them to be happy.
5. Our unifying goal is continuous conscious mastery.
6. Knowledge broad means learning more. Deep means not forgotten but retained permanently.
7. Measure depth by the number of days they can still answer perfectly since last reviewing the material.
8. We utilize our resources so all children continue learning from where they are.
9. Engage the entire class in each one's success. Pair them up so they help each other.

TWO

Sequence Learning Activities Optimally

Arrange a reliable learning system

Our proposed optimal sequence has two phases, Accurate Understanding and Practice to Mastery. First we apprehend and organize knowledge, and then we practice it to mastery. Key activities occur along a timeline, each one expanding students' assimilation of the knowledge.

Accurate Understanding
1. *Input.* "I grasp this."
2. *Analysis.* "I understand what's important about this."
3. *Question and Answer Form.* "I've got this under my control."
Practice to Mastery
4. *Output.* "I can master it."
5. *Mental Movie.* "I have the whole thing inside me."
6. *Score.* "I can tell how well I'm doing."
7. *Performance.* "I can show others I know it."
8. *Spaced Practice.* "I can get even better at it."

Let's look at each step.[1]

1. *Input.* Knowledge arrives at the senses. From kindergarten to graduate school, the means are much the same. Mainly, someone presents it. The teacher shows pictures and talks about them, draws diagrams, shows media material, or explains in detail; then, he or she may engage students in a discussion or pose questions.

Students may gather ideas by reading from a book or handout or from direct experience with projects, devices, field trips, or experiments. Computer programs may lead them through steps, yet their knowledge may still be on the surface, significant jumbled with insignificant.

The amount presented affects later steps. You have to decide how big a chunk to bite off at one time. On the one hand, you want to include more because of expanding interest and meeting curricular checkpoints. On the other, you face the discipline of mastery—two emphases that ideally operate like a wrestling tag team. One advances while the other rests and then they switch. Interest does not suddenly disappear but selects from its mental exploration where to apply discipline of mastery.

Though we would like to run with all the new angles we uncover, unless we limit ourselves to a few, we can be like a gold miner who finds the mother lode and kills himself trying to carry it out. We work with a chunk size students can handle—*a morsel we expect them to chew before biting off more*. A given day's material enters a process assuring its eventual mastery: first understanding it and then organizing it into a form easy to practice.

Having done that, we can safely add more. We need not delay students' first exposure to the next lesson until after this one is learned permanently. Rather, *we pace the succeeding so it does not overwhelm the prior*. In terms of the sequence here, we would do the first four steps for a given lesson—all perhaps in a single hour—before the next lesson is introduced, but we may have several in our pipeline moving through subsequent phases.

2. *Analysis*. Within the knowledge presented, we identify what stands out. If someone speaks to us for ten minutes about an idea, none of us remember it verbatim. We boil down the main idea: "It comes down to this."

The further we expect to carry it, the more selective we are. *What we carry forward will require discipline to assimilate,* so we think about its value, what merits a portion of the finite time and attention available. If this step appears moot because your district has adopted a curriculum, ask yourself: Is every single word in the curriculum *tested*? If not, then selection is involved. If you do not expect verbatim memory, you drop part and save part; You home in on essences.

If choices are possible, you might ask students to help prioritize, assigning them in pairs to select key points, or "read it overnight and be ready to talk about what's important tomorrow," or discuss it in small groups until the important becomes clear. Doing so, students grasp the material in a more organized way. They understand the relative value of the points presented. If asked, they can explain them and select details illustrating the principle involved.

To show that a student knows a math concept, for instance, you might include definitions of related terms, a formula, steps of a problem-solving sequence, and sample problems. Consolidating the material in such a skeleton enables a student to display mastery of it later. In each subject, we identify what we want them to hold on to at least until the end of the school year and give it a boundary.

The use of programmed materials—computerized or paper-and-pencil—poses a question. While we teach essential material precisely, overdefining questions and answers deprives students of the assimilative activity of reflecting on relationships between ideas.

Matching columns, sentence completion, and blanks to fill in may leave nothing to the imagination and nothing to discover, organize, and integrate. Life's perennial issue, "What's important here?" is missing, already answered. Memory replaces judgment. Even lengthy involvement with overspecific, unintegrated material may leave them little knowledge they are able to think about later because their manner of learning did not link knowledge in meaningful networks.

With analysis, the student has learned, sorted, and understood. The material is familiar and briefly exposed to working memory, which most regard as the completion of instruction. They press on to the next unit, ignoring for this one the steps below that convert familiar into permanent learning.

3. *Question and Answer (Q and A) Form.* We next arrange the material in a way that enables students to take it on to mastery.

We *form* Q and A after material has been presented and analyzed. If questions are obvious, you state them yourself to use time well or say, "Let's think what questions best represent what I've explained." The class can brainstorm, throw out suggestions, and agree on one or more; or you arrange students in threes and ask each group to settle on the questions that summarize the content. The groups report back, and the class compiles a preferred list.

Q and A *focuses* the mind. Regardless of how much we eventually want to teach them, we encounter a bottleneck. Children's minds accept one thing at a time. We need a way to identify it and send it along the narrow pathway lodging it deeper. Q and A is the specification of the knowledge we use to elicit it, each of a size students will not choke on.

Q and A helps *represent* the knowledge. Shaping the material this way assembles the pieces into an integrated picture. Speaking it to a partner enables students to *hear* themselves and others. They also need to *see* it formed as images, diagrams, structures, and important words. The kinesthetically inclined appear to benefit when eye-hand-brain come together in manually writing out the questions and answers or applying them *hands-on*—decisive for many children's learning. For ideas presented initially in a computer program, the teacher may wish to identify them and ask students to explain, write, master, and save them.[2]

Writing the Q and A furthermore asserts a value. Identifying words as worth the extra effort, we assure students that they are important enough to practice and carry forward. We point their energy with an answer that distinguishes what to save from what they can leave to chance. Without hard copy, we lack a standard against which to assess our mental model. Writing out answers also makes personal claim more likely. We save what is on *this* piece of paper.

Q and A *completes* the knowledge. When we vaguely remember an answer, it may feel complete even though we forget some of it. Our mind forms a whole, though incorrect, with the remaining pieces. Writing out Q and A defines what we want to save so that we can refresh our lapses and correct our mistakes.

Q and A makes *practice* possible. It casts knowledge in a form students can use to get better at it. Asking and answering the questions, recalling the material repeatedly until it is locked in their brain, they develop mastery. If points are worth saving, we identify and save them by practice, but because this takes time and attention, we cannot do it for everything. We satisfy ourselves with what we deem important.

To help make practice comprehensive, ask students to compile a cumulative list of all the questions you treat, without the answers, titled Final Exam or Total Course. Include every significant point as the course proceeds, and make sure students can competently explain each. If you individualize instruction, let each student use the question they personally derive from the material.

Some object that writing out answers is too much work, that an agency should standardize and print them. In addition to practical problems with that approach, *discerning the key point* is part of understanding. Faced with an array of details, students' minds must labor to tease out, "What's central here? How can we express it in an orderly way?"

Their framing of the issue also reflects how a teacher introduces it and students grasp it. For one class, a preset list would be too burdensome, but for another, too spare, making it complex for some and boring for others. Overspecifying material from the start can turn it into a stream of data lacking a matrix. Instead you want a connected field in which facts cohere as you explain them. Recall and understanding develop partly by organizing relationships between the points presented.

4. *Output*. By the steps above, we present the material, analyze it for its key points, and convert them to questions and answers. Next is the practice enabling the mind to assimilate them.

The axiom "Practice makes perfect" tells why. Degree of skill overall is in proportion to the amount of practice. People of even average ability can develop superior skill just by working at it, and those at the top of any profession, talented or not, typically put in thousands of hours. Teachers who "learn a subject by teaching it" do the same. They explain over and over.

Mastering and using knowledge depends almost entirely on how we express it. We form an internal model and then demonstrate it outwardly. When we present an idea to a student and ask him to explain it back, he may need several tries. His approximations of it may wander far afield before he can explain it accurately. He needs to translate the received impression into word meanings he knows.

Besides building skill, practice in explaining *also implies relationship*; two people, one asking and the other answering. We mesh practice with social values. Students pair up, ask each other the questions, and certify each other's ability, aligning with their tendency to regard relationships as significant even if they were not previously friends. They innately want to be viewed as competent by their peers. If they are to express learning, they want to do it well.

Whatever you want them to become good at, have them practice it with another student who then declares, "He did it." Divide complex material into chunks: "Explain it to your partner piece by piece and make sure you both know all the pieces." In this phase you can also utilize students who grasp the idea first. Send them around the class explaining it to any who need help.

For students to practice alone, ask them to re-organize in writing everything they know.[3] Comprehending ideas, recognizing how they connect, and putting them in well-chosen words is a lifetime skill they will use often but develop only by practice.

5. *Mental movie.* Much learning is available through the imagination. If you took a child to a movie and afterward offered him a dollar a minute for narrating it, how long could he talk? With a weekly challenge like that, he would quickly tap out the family entertainment budget. Because most people are visually oriented, they easily remember anything packaged as a story. Random ideas are harder to keep in mind, so present them with imagery, sequence, and structure if you can. Too many isolated facts, rules, and general statements neutralize imagination.

You might rethink your material according to how you would present it if it were in a movie plot. *Sequence is an organizing principle.* Draw on it in a discussion by inviting students to connect with the comment just made: "Summarize what was said before adding your own."

What may stick most easily is not that Thomas Jefferson wrote the Declaration of Independence but that their friend Eric said so. Facts spontaneously link to continuing experience. The imagery containing all their learning came to them effortlessly but is rapidly discarded unless soon called on.[4]

Once a day tell students, "Close your eyes, go inside, and run today's movie in as much detail as you can remember. Include everything you learned in the order you learned it." Do this also at the end of any content-rich period. When your class watches a media program, pause it every quarter hour, discuss the questions and answers it treated (steps 1–3 above), and do Mental Movie with that portion.

With lessons previously mastered, regular use of Mental Movie may be the most efficient way to maintain and deepen them. The method is easy to use, trains students in concentration, and fits into brief time slots.

You might initially lead them through an experience at a pace you find comfortable for forming each step yourself:

> Let's begin with an imagination trip so you see how easy this is. Close your eyes and get comfortable. Imagine yourself in a movie theater. Nod your head when you've done that. . . . Notice where you're sitting in the theater and how big the screen looks. Run your eye up the left edge of it . . . across the top . . . down the right side . . . and across the bottom. . . . Nod when you've done that. If it's hard for you to see pictures, follow the sequence by its sounds or actions. Lights are still on in the theater, and then they dim. . . . Hear music playing in the background. . . . See the title appearing. . . .

Take them through familiar images such as walking up to the school in the morning, forming each scene. Run their imagining eye along the edge of the features of the building, feel the smooth door handle; hear their feet on the steps, cars in the background, and friends' greetings. Include sound, sight, and touch. Pace their movement as though looking through a camera lens. Call attention to a zone but let them invent the detail. After you lead them a little, say, "Just continue the movie as it unfolds. Go from one hour of your day to the next and focus where your attention is drawn. Remember all the details in turn that we have discussed and everything we have done so far today."

After a bit, some will open their eyes, or you can ask them to end in a half-minute. For fun, complete it like a movie:

> The film winds down and the credits scroll up the screen. Add your name after each category: script by, directed by, produced by, casting by—all by your name. Film ends, lights come back on, and you're sitting in the theater. The big screen is blank. Notice how it felt to run your own movie.

Debrief the experience. How many continued the scene after you stopped guiding it? Check for unexpected images or events, feelings arising, what they heard, how things felt to the touch, whether images seemed close or far away. Identifying qualities of their scene helps them take control of encoding knowledge later.

6. *Score*. With accurate scoring we track what reaches our criterion of mastery and separate it from what does not. We count up each piece of learning that does.

Why score. We presume that every course contains knowledge worth retaining permanently, worth the effort of saving it, and does not leave that core chunk to chance. To make sure we save it, we keep count of it, we monitor the pieces known and unknown in order to guide the next effort: "You got most of the alphabet but are missing m, n, and o." We track each discrete unit and, piece by piece, home in on what is important to us.

Such a commitment represents a policy change for much of American education. Some students have substantial knowledge gaps; often for years no one has paid attention to their grasp of key details—a third grade girl who could not recall the number between three and five, an eighth grade boy never taught the vowel sounds.

If we once create a criterion for mastery, the next logical step is to score the learning reaching that level. This encourages students. They realize that their effort with a specific piece has succeeded. They appreciate scoring that matches their conscious effort and keeps them on a track to improvement.

Displaying the report of their effort further enhances motivation. Scores posted publicly beside their name become socially significant. They compare themselves to their peers and want to show up well. If the scale is in objective numbers that they can change rapidly with more work at learning, they are stimulated to do that.

Scoring encourages ownership. As students count up their answers accurately, they realize they can monitor their retention of everything they know. Reserving a score only for consciously retained knowledge means that if asked the question, they can demonstrate the answer *any time,* giving them an objective basis for pride and confidence. Their numerical count of their progress coincides with what they know they can do because they can call it up right then.

What to score. For identifying the content deserving a score, a criterion both valid and reliable is *the ability to tell back learning without help.* If you wait for that to occur before assigning a score, you eliminate half-baked answers and forms of questioning that hint at the answer or that an astute test-taker may figure out: multiple choice, true/false, sentence completion, matching columns, or assignments that ask students to duplicate a source—means that supply superficial practice but stop short of competence. Constantly depending on external clues to assemble their knowledge weakens their confidence in the power of their mind.

We regard as mastered instead what is lodged comprehensively in the brain, and we specify parts if we can: "There were five steps to the process and you got them all for a score of five," adding five to the student's total for that section. Since each integer means a student claims to know a specific piece continuously, we do not score again for that piece but expect the first to be retained permanently. In the times tables of 9s up to ninety are ten increments of progress. Students telling them all to a partner deserve the maximum count, and for any products forgotten, their score is reduced accordingly. A single cumulative number totals up all the learning they claim to know.

In the upper grades, questions are often more complex with multiple parts, steps, or features taken into account. To score them, think parallel to constructing a test. We give separate value to increments of an answer representing independent work if we can. If a part requires effort to learn (is not embedded within or implied by another), it deserves a score. If when missed it would be marked off on a test but is correct, it deserves a score. In "getting that piece right," a student is pleased that his effort paid off and encouraged to do the same with another.

By scoring every part of an answer that took independent effort to learn, we make the charted score reflect actual effort. It reports validly their output of energy on questions having many parts compared to those with only one and applies to material of all kinds.[5]

7. *Performance*. In performance, we demonstrate to others a skill worth displaying. It contains motivational impact little utilized in standard education, combining *mastery* and *pleasure* in one experience. Cultural messages surround it: significance, celebration, excitement, ability, effort, applause, and the spotlight. Performance puts a rocket under pedestrian-level approval. No matter what they perform, that thimbleful of minutes in any week is sure to preoccupy them. It hits them that something representing them deserves admiring attention.

Teachers tend to regard learning instead as solitary, that students one by one grasp ideas, but this brings them just to the doorway where excitement begins. If teachers do not recognize the importance of students *enjoying* their mastery, they skip it and proceed to the next unit.

To engage energy, once a day for a few minutes make a game out of performance by 1) placing in a bag a slip for every question they can answer, 2) drawing a question, and 3) drawing a name. Then, 4) the student rises, since standing enhances significance, and answers the question, and 5) others applaud. In *Effective Classroom Turnaround: Practice Makes Permanent* is an explanation of how a periodic evening public performance can carry a gamelike quality, draw on the entire curriculum, increase interest, include students of varying ability, and ensure everyone's success.

8. *Spaced practice*. With prior steps done well, the final question is whether or not to make the learning permanent. Spaced practice offers the fastest route once students have a complete correct answer. Devote regular time, such as a period a week, for partner practice on all questions back to the beginning of the term, and vary the effort at times with Mental Movie.

While on the face of it this last step sounds like a good idea, it contradicts current custom and implies uncommon outcomes for education. Too many educators' target for the year is enough familiarization to pass students to the next grade or earn credits.

Check whether this applies to you. Last year, did it satisfy you to move your students on to the next checkpoint? Or were you also thinking, "I'm *adamant* that they master this"? Which standard does your system expect of you? To which does the activity of you and your students logically lead?

The picture above contains the basics. However we innovate, we still need to *input information, analyze it for what to carry forward, convert it into questions and answers, master them, plot progress objectively, and sink the information deep enough that it stays.* With this sequence as a yardstick, we can estimate the likely success of other methods. To the extent that they contain these steps, they should produce deep learning.

TESTING POINTS

The approach itself is not hard to apply, but because it diverges from usual procedures, it may require persistence to adopt. Introducing it into an existing system, you may need to understand it intimately so you can explain it to others. Here are a few likely testing points.

Testing Point 1. Few teachers understand how even hard work and difficult assignments and "rigor" may still produce superficial knowledge. Plotted from performance at scheduled moments, even high scores can represent knowledge quickly forgotten. *Explain how deep knowledge is obtained.*

Testing Point 2. Society accepts familiarized knowledge as an adequate outcome of an hour's effort. Because this expectation is so minimal yet widespread, the sort of mastery we propose here may appear alien to many. We define mastery as *a student's ability to explain everything he or she knows without help and maintain it,* and short of that, do not refer to it as mastery. *Defend explainable mastery as the outcome.*

Testing Point 3. Many students coast but believe they succeed anyway. They think by showing up and doing minimal assignments they are on track to graduate. They disengage inwardly because they see no good reason for significant effort and may conclude that pushing themselves applies only to the few days before an important test. Instead, *mastered learning depends on continuous effort.*

Testing Point 4. Deciding to master knowledge, we define it specifically. Students need to understand a field of thought but then master the details of its structure that convey the field to others. We *grasp* the field but then *practice* the details that *sustain* the field so we can *explain* it accurately. Just understanding it is not enough. They *master the details that make the field come alive* so they can competently explain the whole subject.

Testing Point 5. To practice and learn something, we write it down, yet writing involves extra effort. Both teachers and students may resist this due to years of tolerating vague learning—teachers because they want to cover more, and students because of expecting only to touch on the material anyway, so why write it.

Yet without hard copy they keep, they cannot correct their errors, cannot practice effectively, and do not save it as well. The physical act rivets learning in place and claims for them the details to practice. Those who find writing difficult might work with a concise handout, or a student or parent can help as scribe. *Insist on hard copy.*

Testing Point 6. Consider the present ideas as a chunk of knowledge. How much effort would it cost you to assimilate the contents of this book well enough to use it *without referring to it*? Calculate that and apply the parallel to your subject. What will it take for your students to learn your text deeply enough to apply it without opening it? *Ask for disciplined thought.*

Testing Point 7. Realize what happens when students no longer forget what they learn. Imagine a single question appropriate for your students of any level. It has five parts in the answer. Imagine that in one hour you explain it, organize it neatly, and everyone writes it down. They practice explaining the five parts to a partner, master and save them, and refresh prior learning.

Following out that average template generates an amazing outcome. Saving 5 answer points every 60 minutes for 5 instructional hours a day comes to 25 points a day. But do the math. At that pace, 180 school days times 25 points per day totals 4,500 points. Done another way, 180 days times 5 hours a day equals 900 class hours a year. Learning 5 points per hour for 900 hours totals 4,500. *Adding 25 points a day for a school year comes to 4,500 points!*

If that sounds too aggressive, cut it in half. Learn 5 points every 2 instructional hours and you still have 2,250 points for the year. What matters is not how much passes through students' minds *but how much pauses there. Explain the power of steady accumulation.*

For mastering quantities of knowledge, two activities are indispensable: 1) identify the knowledge worth saving, and 2) carry out the discipline of saving it.[6] To do this, align with the brain's manner of absorbing knowledge: understand it, select what's important to save, define it in words, organize it by question and answer, and practice it at spaced intervals until it is assimilated into permanent knowledge.

SUMMARY

1. We can optimize the steps leading to mastery.
2. Children must first accurately grasp an idea.
3. Pace the succeeding so it does not overwhelm the prior.
4. Important must be separated from unimportant.
5. Cast important knowledge in question and answer form.
6. For deep assimilation, students output the knowledge to each other.
7. Deepen retention by running the mental movie of their learning.
8. Score it objectively by whether they remember it continually.
9. Students perform it to the class.

10. They re-explain the knowledge in pairs at spaced intervals.

11. Teachers may need to explain how deep knowledge is obtained, defend explainable mastery as the outcome, ask for continuous effort, master details, insist on hard copy, and ask for disciplined thought.

12. Learning 5 new points per instructional hour results in 4,500 points for the school year.

NOTES

1. Cossondra George, "Teaching Secrets: Teaching Students How to Learn," *Education Week Teacher* (online), July 19, 2011. George provides helpful details that apply to steps 2–4 here: how to identify main ideas, note-taking, ways to practice and memorize, and how to recognize progress.

2. An emphasis of Neuro-Linguistic Programming (NLP) is drawing on the full range of children's manner of representing knowledge. While research has not supported full-blown learning styles, all of us may *represent* an idea as a picture, a sound, or an action. A child may prefer one of these modes and appear to reveal his or her current processing of a thought through eye movements that access the brain differently. Looking at the ceiling, for instance, children typically examine a mental picture. For a day's lesson, we increase the likelihood of everyone grasping it by using visual, auditory, and kinesthetic means. Over-reliance on a single instructional method probably limits flexibility of thought formation.

3. Adam Robinson, *What Smart Students Know: Maximum Grades. Optimum Learning. Minimum Time* (New York: Three Rivers Press, 1993). Robinson explains how important is a students' own synthesis of learning in his own words, a principle that also applies in society. We are constantly asked to comprehend an issue and make sense of it to others with well-chosen words.

4. The speed of discard of new information from working memory is well documented. See several references in *Teaching Students to Work Harder and Enjoy It: Practice Makes Permanent*. The process of sorting what to retain from what to discard occurs in microseconds usually spontaneous and automatic. Writing out the material reinstructs the brain to change this automatic activity into a deliberate one: "About this material, I'm not going to discard it."

5. Teachers do not score most scientific and mathematical problems this way. Typically a single correct answer validates all the steps leading up to it, but this fails to acknowledge the differential energy students expend in learning one solution compared to another. In a ten-step sequence, each step takes effort. To encourage it by the manner of scoring is not a mainstream objective, even though staff may wonder why students "aren't motivated." For it to matter more to them, match increments of correct effort with tallies of score. The final answer of the sequence is almost incidental compared to the effort expended to get there. To help students, we count up the effort of the steps leading to the outcome.

6. Much of what we need in education mirrors what we need in society. The point I make here parallels the formula for success attributed to Nelson Bunker Hunt: 1) Decide what you want. 2) Determine its price. 3) Pay the price.

THREE

Arrange for Good Feelings

Why bring balance to students' feelings

MEET THE NEEDS PRESENTED

Veteran teachers know the power of children's feelings and find ways to work with them, but even they are occasionally hosed with a realization they had not fully appreciated. Consider first graders preparing for a class activity. The teacher gives them full-throated admonishment for talking out of turn and not paying attention, yet the sheer urgency and enthusiasm of their feelings drives them. A comment by teacher or classmate spurs a thought and they are impelled to declare it to the class despite consequences that might fall upon them. They *have* to say this, but their teacher, determined to maintain a quiet classroom, quells their expressiveness. Quiet students *a priori* are considered better students. Once more it becomes obvious how much better we can do to address students' emotional needs. If we want to teach effectively, we must consider the affective domain.

An assumption about this is not universally shared—that we should acknowledge the condition of the student arriving at our door and set about meeting the needs presented; that we should refuse to operate in an imaginary world populated by students different from ours. We accept them as they walk in and educate them regardless of the impact of home conditions on their learning.[1] Excuses for not remedying their deficits consign them to a lifetime of deficit. Schools are meant to enable children to make it in life despite what their parents failed to supply.

We begin below, arguing against a belief that feelings and attitudes do not matter. Then we discuss the teacher as plug-in, the drawback of anger, the power of teacher beliefs, the link between feelings and learning in

19

depth, the function of safety, and feelings as signal. In the next chapter, we look at classroom activities.

THE SIGNIFICANCE OF FEELINGS AND ATTITUDES

Many teachers dismiss the importance of feelings and attitudes as long as students function in class. They think that both positive and negative feelings can threaten order and interfere with learning. Addressing them may seem a divergence and, since doing so can consume entire days if we allow it, are not we better off requiring students to suppress them?

No, we are not. In fact, let me trouble your sleep. Would it make a difference to you that even in elementary school you could tell that certain students were headed for a *lifetime* of trouble? And that how you personally deal with their attitudes may influence them for decades?

Forty years ago, Kohlberg, LaCross, and Ricks found a common theme among prior longitudinal studies. *The two best predictors of all forms of adult maladjustment were poor peer relations in the first three grades of school and antisocial behavior in the second three grades.*[2]

A kindergarten teacher may already cope with inconsiderateness and pushing. By fifth grade the boy has developed a secretive mean streak and occasionally manifests aggressiveness. In the tenth grade staff suspect him of minor sabotage around the school, and at twenty-three, he breaks the law. The criminal justice system lays its hand on his shoulder and says to him, "Too bad, Bud. You should have listened to your kindergarten teacher. Your road is now with us!" and Bud cannot quite comprehend what has seized him. Even to preserve itself, society is wise to attend to early indicators.[3]

Any reasonable accounting should show that happy, successful children learn better and that we waste more time coping with their bad feelings than we would spend to generate good ones. Positive feelings and attitudes are a net gain for learning. For those worried about time lost from academics to address students' social/emotional/behavioral needs, a review of 213 studies about the value of such instruction lends reassurance. Following are some conclusions.

Children receiving such instruction improved their academic standing by 11 percentage points with greater social skills, less emotional stress, and better attitudes. They had fewer conduct problems, such as bullying and suspensions, and more frequent positive behaviors, such as cooperation and help for other students.

Best approaches were classroom based and teacher led rather than more elaborate programs and were sequenced step-by-step, enabled students to be active, had sufficient time focused on each lesson, and aimed at explicit learning goals. Effective time on task increased by as much as 40 percent.[4]

The first group the Kohlberg study noted—kids up to grade three relating poorly to peers—is typically desperate to cope with the world. These students gladly try to understand the clues we provide. Their problem is "us." We do not know what to say to them about the feelings that oppress them except, "Get over it!" Fear, loneliness, anger, envy, resentment, and sadness depress their motivation and skew their behavior. Few have the capacity simply to apply good advice.

Satisfying their need for attention is typically for them the meaning of giving the right answer. They thread their schoolwork through a tangle of feelings. A sense of lack, of being invisible, ignored, lonely, anxious, and uncertain clogs up the working memory they rely on to absorb new knowledge.

Feeling alone and invisible bleaches out values. Important truths are deflated just to empty words. Worth drains away, leaving us puzzled why a child with ample resources and tangible successes cannot claim and build on them. A half-century-old comment explains: *Children are a speck of intelligence in a sea of emotion.* If we do not reach them in the affective dimension, we may not reach them at all.

Students in the second three years of school exhibiting antisocial behavior are a rebuke for the time we wasted when turning them around could have been easy. By upper elementary, behaviors are more entrenched, stakes higher, and change harder. Now we must navigate the labyrinth of their mind for what propels their actions and modify it in time for them to survive in society.

FEELINGS AID GROWTH

Feelings matter not only overall but also in critical niches in children's growth parallel to infant development. In one period they can learn hundreds of new words a day. If no one speaks around them, it leaves a gap. They want to begin using their hands, but what if they may not hold anything? Needing to feel safe to explore the world—a room, the front yard—what if they face only scolding and threat for doing so? Again, a gap.

Comparable feeling-based tools children rely on to cope with the world can be fractured. They receive rejection when they need acceptance, threat when they need safety, silence when they need communication, neutrality when they need challenge, isolation when they need presence, routine when they need variety, compliance when they need initiative, limitation when they need creativity.

The gaps would matter less if children could just override them. Instead they may fuse with children's picture of the world and structure of their brain. Their real world may be etched in rejection, threat, isolation, silence, compliance, and limitation. These conditions don't come together like a photo on a page they can turn, or a movie they can eject from their DVD player.

A closer parallel might be *extracting one of our own teeth* when a toothache will not quit. The version of self we absorb reconfigures our brain, requiring great determination or significant help to alter it. As we grow, we carry with us the unsatisfactory emotional plans we developed as children, as though depositing them on a shelf for later use when similar conditions arise.

In our adult lives they suddenly show up when circumstances conspire. We may expect affection from someone and discover they are angry with us. Our good feelings disappear, and we are shocked to realize that we must defend ourselves, are thrust suddenly into managing bad feelings. Even though our rationality may urge us otherwise, our animal brain with its built-in defensive reactions may take over, and bad feelings drive us back to strategies we used when we had those feelings before, even if they failed us then.[5]

One might note that poor peer relations and antisocial behavior are actions rather than feelings and inquire why focus on the latter. The actions do not stand alone. Something propels them. Rational thinking is not their source—by definition the actions are inappropriate. But if thinking is irrational, we must ask why. Seldom is the problem a lack of information. Schools lecture students constantly about what they should think and do. Any child behaving antisocially by the fourth grade has heard corrections scores of times.

FEELINGS AFFECT GROUP BEHAVIOR

The most likely source of students' inappropriate behavior is from emotions that narrow thinking. Even good ones can do that by focusing us more intently, driving us toward a desired thing or away from an undesired. As adults, we expect knowledge to give us better judgment, but even in us, emotion can distort our comprehensive knowledge especially when we experience it with a group. A nascent gang has power even in grade school where emotions may be a badge of belonging. To know your allies, just hate and love the same things.

The power of emotion in group behavior is a vulnerability of society making children's affective development particularly urgent. Its impact on mainstream thinking was starkly demonstrated in last century's nationalism and the geopolitics of hate and fear that caught up good people. A Jewish elder recounted how even he, as a teenager in Germany in the 1930s, found the Nazi's parades, rallies, and music attractive. With thousands of male voices in marching cadence expressing confidence and triumph, who would not want to belong? Group emotion offers connection, and rationales follow to justify the feelings.

We bring health to group emotion by balanced management of it and not merely by suppression. Even though their messages can be mischanneled, emotions somehow provide a visceral grip on fundamental values.[6] The meaning embedded in emotion can aid the mind but also mislead it because its messages are simple, arising from the primitive brain we share with lower vertebrates, organically distinct from our thinking cortex and following its own elemental logic. One observer compared the messages we receive simultaneously from mind and emotions to overlapping TV signals. We have to choose which to focus on or how to mesh them.

Doing this with balance is harder than it might seem. The emotional brain is less concerned with evidence than is the cortex but instead values its sensations so much that its own internal field becomes the reality. *Emotions dominate thinking more easily than the reverse.* Effort is uphill as we direct our brain to steer our feelings. It can take all the willpower we possess to shift gears from even a superficial emotion to a more substantial thought.

Yet when we use this field constructively, we more accurately apprehend others' joy, sorrow, suffering, and hope—enlarging our awareness of them and how we are connected to them. Celebrities and performers engage our emotions in order to connect to us.

Because emotions help create meaning, *if we want something to matter to students, we had best not wring the emotion out of it.* It is appropriate for them to have strong feelings about important things, but unmanaged, experienced randomly, with their tone distorting evidence, emotions can override fact, call white black and truth false; call self-destructive pretty, criminal behavior successful, school boring, teachers oppressive, and peers odd.

The natural fonts of knowing the worth of things can be polluted with misinformation and laden with self-interest and arrogance. Yet our internal system can also establish solid convictions when personal feelings and rational assessment align, when both heart and mind absorb a full range of data pointing to the same conclusion.

We encourage moderate emotion in the classroom both by how we express our own and how we design their experience. If we fail to teach them to see past their superficial reactions, few learn it by themselves. Emotions lurch through their lives even though by luck the majority contain them within legal limits. Their lingering presence for good or ill means we cannot afford just to dismiss or suppress them.

TEACHER AS PLUG-IN

We readily forget how unnatural classroom activity can be. Imagine that you teach high school social studies and one of your students is your son's best friend who is often at your house. Even though you are careful not to allow him any special break in class, your link with him is different, not from favoritism or liking but from an ontological aspect.

In both your minds, *a reality persists,* and the classroom simply extends it. Other students think they "have you" for social studies, and outside the class you recede to a remote figure in their mind.

In your living room, what do you assume when an adult enters? 1) All are significant. No one is left out. 2) You as host have a personal relationship to everyone. You treat them with respect as guests and include them in anything that occurs. 3) Since everyone matters, when one speaks others listen, and all sustain stable connections. Everyone expects face-to-face response, acceptance, agreements fulfilled, and respectful, inclusive conversation.

Now match your classroom to your living room. Your students deserve just such treatment. If teachers do not generate such conditions at school where students spend much of their lives, an objective observer would deem it unnatural, not one a rational person would choose. Adults would extricate themselves quickly. While the college dynamic differs slightly, legitimate human connections there increase the relevance of the class. With learning a way students bond with each other, even arcane knowledge becomes a primordial bridge.

We extend this bridge to students first through our solidity, our presence, our face-to-face reality in their eyes. How we manage ourselves is the template for what we create in them, but transmitting it may not be easy in a setting designed only for outer actions. We may have power to give a grade or apply a consequence, but if the student writes us off as a person, a range of learning goes missing.

Personally significant to them, we return to our basic connection whenever things go awry, just as we would in our own living room. We resume eye-to-eye contact, a respectful tone, and a calm demeanor. We reset back to our visceral presence, ask for the student's attention, and *they enter our consciousness,* they "plug in" to our picture of reality.

Children reveal much about themselves through their eyes, and the younger they are, the more uncensored their gaze is. Looking straight on, they may catch their teacher's full bore, declaring wordlessly, "I love you." Ordered about as they are from morning until night, they nonetheless give adults the benefit of the doubt, hoping we will be a light in their world and do more than control them.

Many arrive habituated to an impersonal or polarized view of the classroom. If they at first lump us with other teachers who treat them as objects, we become a pivotal cause as we determine to be different. Like welcoming guests to our living room, we offer them the substance of our personal presence though they may not recognize it at once. For a time even in our home, our child's friend may be ill at ease until confident of his connection with us.

Provide students an easy way to connect to you personally. One effective teacher made sure to offer a personal, private comment to everyone each day. Some teachers admit students to the classroom one at a time to shake hands and exchange a smile or thought. Face to face, you can satisfy yourself that they expect to cooperate. Some may need to reaffirm an agreement: "I'm ready to learn," or "I'll ask permission before I speak," or "I'm going to have a good day," acknowledging the behavior that makes the difference. A few may need an extra minute of attention after others enter.

Each student should know that you are steadily aware of good things about them and can direct a stream of accurate comments toward them: "And you, Jerry, what I (respect, appreciate, admire) about you is . . . I've seen you do . . . and I notice . . . and here you're already doing . . ." Their every learning task has an advancing point to it, and how they negotiate it right now is significant: "Ah, you got that detail!" No details are smaller than a single period, but its location is important: "Yes! You got the period in the right place." Recognizing their leading-edge details sustains their sense of continuing success.

Through the day, watch for moments when you can nurture the connection, especially with a student whose behavior wanders. You might draw him to you: "Stay for a minute, would you?" Face him longer, invite eye contact, and ask, "Are you ready to focus on learning or do you need more time with me?" Notice their cues. If you are uncertain about their state, keep them beside you until assured that they are ready to work at a distance.

When their behavior tells you that their relationship with you has weakened, restore it immediately: "Michael, please come and sit with me." Michael remains wired to you until his battery is charged up enough that he can function again on his own. Present this personally close time not as punishment but as focus: "Relax. It's okay. Just watch what we're doing until you're ready to work." Never hold it against them that they have broken a rule. Harboring a bad feeling about a student amounts to a self-fulfilling prophecy of future misbehavior.

THE DRAWBACK OF ANGER

The biggest threat to your link with them is your anger. Understand it. Anger increases what you hope is others' perception of your power so they will comply with what you want. Frequent anger at children reveals negative beliefs about human nature—that people do not respond to reason and are not oriented to the good and that your intelligence and character are not enough.

If they were, you think, students would do what you tell them, but they do not so you must resort to negative means. Though you prefer a positive view of human nature, it seems irrelevant to the conditions you face, so you shift gears and act as though human nature were negative. Good luck with that viewpoint. You have much support in U.S. criminal justice policies that incarcerate 2.3 million people, many ironically "enrolled in schools for crime." We reveal our values most obviously by the conditions we impose on those under our power.

When you become angry, at least do not defend it as right. The truth is that you have failed to influence them through your goodness and firmness, and so resort instead to negative power. That we can do better was illustrated by a gentle psychologist who earlier in her life had spent eleven years as a guard in a women's prison.

"In all those years," she said, "I *never* had anyone say or do anything nasty toward me. They knew I *respected* them."

Confronting a problem, any of us may be upset, feel misunderstood, and impose our attitude on others, but we need not clutch at it nor build a worldview justifying it. Your frustration should alert you that you do not know how to do something. If anyone anywhere in the world could handle your situation smoothly, a learning opportunity stands before you.

When conditions elicit your anger or frustration, aim at problem solving with fascination. Reorient your feelings: "Something is going wrong here. I don't know yet how to handle it. I'm going to try some things and am fascinated at what I'll learn." Apologize, admit your difficulty in dealing with the situation, try to see others as equally significant at the personal if not the role level, and attempt to talk out the issue humbly.

Such an attitude displaces the tendency to apply labels that injure students. Even for us adults, many hurts begin just with others judging us. They declare a standard to be important and that we do not measure up, and their anger literally hurls their verdict at us. To a criticism closing in on us, we are typically on our guard and retreat to a hurt, position of defense, or to self-limitation.

One might protest, "So what?" Life can be tough, circumstances jar us, we cope, and children should do the same. But we handle others' judgments best when solidly confident of our worth. Developmentally, children may be at a turning point when they especially need others' acceptance. When that need is in question, teachers' critical opinion of them pulls them down, diminishes them, dismisses them as unworthy. Their behavior may be so obviously bad that the teacher feels a label is justified. Imagine! Children talk in class when told not to!

We ask them to "Shape up!" yet discount them and drive them into a defensive posture so that they use up their energy just fending off our ill regard for them. Grappling with their unmet needs, they have less energy for learning. In nearly any repeated problem, a basic emotion is misdirected. The more we free them from hurts and limitations, the more their minds operate from natural zest and intelligence.

THE POWER OF TEACHER BELIEFS

We might inquire why teachers apply negative labels to students at all, since this appears to be a free choice. To understand why, we examine teacher beliefs. Decades ago the University of Florida sponsored a series of research projects, one of them to find out what distinguished good teachers. It proceeded in a novel fashion.[7]

To define valid comparison groups, researchers asked incoming freshmen at Florida colleges to name their best and worst K–12 teachers. Those repeatedly and unanimously described one way or the other formed two sets—all in one were regarded as worst, and in the other, best.

Some may object that students are not objective judges of teacher quality, and in the heat of a conflict, they might not be. Yet given time and reflection on a teacher's true impact, their collective agreement is probably as valid a standard as we can devise. If any of us had been among those college freshmen, would we have any doubt that we could answer unerringly and tell their names even now decades later?

The researchers invited the two groups to participate in a study about teaching. Their first set of questions revealed that the good ones did not know more than the poor. Almost all tests given could not distinguish between them. Extra years of education did not help, a discovery that could have yielded valuable insights had it been followed up.

At the time, the value of strict classroom control was argued. To check this out, they observed classrooms to divide teachers by their degree of "structure." Still this did not separate the groups. The good or bad might or might not be structured and push students. They dug into teachers' thinking. How did they view what they were doing?

Here at last the sample divided. The best had positive beliefs about their frame of reference, people, self, and the teaching task. The worst had negative beliefs in those categories, with the two groups occupying opposite poles on some twenty dimensions. *Their belief caused some to get excellent results from the same activity that gave others poor results.*

The good/frees, for example, believed that kids would find their own way, but the poor/frees believed that they would not learn anyway, so why try? The good/structured believed they *could* learn so pushed them, while the poor/structured believed they *could not* learn so you *have to* push them. Students felt the impact of the belief teachers drew on, whether they personally applied positive or negative labels.

The study has staggering implications not assimilated into American educational thought. It tells the hiring office that it really matters how teachers generate meaning and bids administrators watch how they color the classroom atmosphere. While a few of us may be very good or bad, most of us carry a spectrum of beliefs and may fortuitously draw from one end or the other. We can identify the motives arising in our heart, savor their essence, and apply the better—possessing at least a measure of choice over the belief we act on.

If a voice inside you defends your negativity, saying, "Well, I *have to* be this way," an alternative does exist. In your mind, going negative probably means you think you manage them better. You use the labels that seem to justify your intimidating or ignoring them.

Instead you might distinguish *firm* from *negative.* A clue to which of these you use is whether or not you *like* students. You can be firm but still positive, apply even severe discipline yet retain your bond with them, appreciate their personal enthusiasm and good will more than you object to their unmanaged impulses.

And if any other teacher in the world could conduct your class positively, you simply have more to learn. Do not make excuses that amount to blaming students. If you do not know how to channel their effort into learning, get help. Probe how your students think about classroom order. People who value others value how they think. Harsh words and threats may obtain temporary compliance, but your goal is their understanding. As a full human being to them, you explain your intent and expect that they will respond to it:

> I can't teach you unless I can help you focus. If you want to do X and I say it's time to do Y, I can be constantly working against your thinking. Unless I can refocus you, we get nowhere. There's nothing basically wrong with 99 percent of what you want to do. You talk with friends, make jokes, and want to be playful. These things are good and you'll do them the rest of your life. But if you want to learn, I have to be able to focus you.

Your tone of voice matters. Think how one of the better Florida teachers would speak the paragraph above. They would expect students to take it to heart, and the tone would be considerate and firm, yet inviting. From a worse Florida teacher, the same words would sound whiney or sarcastic, like a complaint or accusation.

FEELINGS AFFECT DEPTH

Students give a stream of clues about their feelings, so you can put a name to the one they appear to have and notice how your personal influence affects it. How you help them *feel* leads directly to how they will *feel about learning,* which influences the depth to which they pursue it. We want to instill good feelings about the process rather than require them to override bad ones.

We start off life believing that everything is new, fresh, and exciting. Repeating experiences makes them more common, and after the newness wears off we need a different reason for doing them. But think about it.

Learning continually pushing into the unknown *is intrinsically new* and deserves a steady sense of freshness. Curiosity alerts us to things we want to take for our own, saying, "Grab hold of this! Make it yours!" A kid seeing a pretty rock puts it in his pocket to take home and show someone.

He takes home an idea by mastering it. Curiosity draws students to the new flavor, but satisfaction arises from chewing and swallowing it. Their thought changes from "How interesting!" to "I'm getting better." If the feeling attached to the new knowledge instead is boredom or burden, it can only be because we deliver it under conditions robbing its natural appeal. Children lack the adult ability to override negative circumstances, so it hobbles their education to conclude that once curiosity wears off, *the only thing left is work and don't expect to enjoy it.*

It increases students' pleasure at learning as 1) they notice that personal effort generates competence, and 2) they can demonstrate it to peers who appreciate it. Any activity done as a group can be designed to meet social needs, build social skills, and engage good feelings. We gain competence with the knowledge first by the effort of learn, save, learn, save, and then we endow it with social value by demonstrating it to others, counting each piece saved as a success. When we count only incremental success and arrange effort to achieve it, we have no need to count failure.

THE FUNCTION OF SAFETY

The usual way people resolve unhappy feelings is to talk them out with a safe and interested listener. Many occupations offer to help us do this. Considering the urgency of their needs and their inability to understand (much less balance) their feelings, children are terribly undersupplied with such help. They turn first to parents, but the latter's need to discipline and their tendency to scold bad behavior can make them appear less safe to talk to.

A safe atmosphere has long been regarded as a basic precondition for how schools help children. Physical safety is essential but not enough. To sustain their confidence, children need to know that they will not be violated, that their school experience will not tear them down. They need emotional safety. Current attention to verbal bullying by peers signals a larger need, *children's management of their inner world.*

To open their world for thoughtful reconsideration, we have to get past an instinctive protection. Calling up issues to address openly presumes *an unconscious sense of safety.* With it well established, we probe better the thoughts that could upset us, such as facing mistakes and examining attitudes that led to them.

None of us willingly brings to mind issues that make us feel guilty or helpless or that challenge the basic assumptions of our identity or threaten our good feelings. If we were wrong, or hurt or misled someone, our internal censor screens out the material from arising in our thoughts until we feel confident enough to grapple with it. And if we are like this just owning up to our own limitations, we are much more so facing them before others.

Adults seeking control over us side with the threatening voices already alive in us and give them force. As they scrutinize us, critical and complaining, we instinctively know we must first defend ourselves. Our guard is up as long as we believe we could be wounded, and with our attention devoted to threat, our self-healing capacities of consciousness are not free to do their work. We cannot disclose the challenges of our inner world to others who draw down our good feelings. First we make sure we are not vulnerable, and only then can we ponder how to bring up what we need to talk about.

A direct correlation exists *between our sense of safety, and the significance of the material we address voluntarily.* The safer we feel, the deeper we can go. To the extent that students are not emotionally safe, *they feel isolated,* unable to express their genuine feelings and masking them instead. Most of us grapple with safety unconsciously, estimating how much, with this person at this moment, we can afford to express. The safer everyone is in our classroom, the more they can resolve their urgent issues and listen to what we say.

FEELINGS AS SIGNAL

Besides their importance for children's development, a reason serving adults in their vicinity is that *feelings constitute a signal* driving the behaviors that concern adults most. A feeling judges the world and tells a student to do the action implied in it. Fear tells us to flee, love tells us to connect, jealousy tells us to eliminate a rival, hurt tells us to protect ourselves, sadness tells us to grieve, and so on.

Managing a feeling becomes harder as its message bypasses the conscious mind and hypnotizes us into patterned behavior. Left to themselves, feelings can grow unobtrusively so that we sense, for example, that we want to get away from a particular place. Our animal brain may process details escaping our conscious mind, presenting us finally with a full-blown feeling pushing upon us.

Nuances of experience can make a feeling-signal more complex. Resentment sizes up its situation to conclude, "I'm being pushed," "I want to hold my ground," and "I'm angry about it" all at the same time. As interpretations darken, it becomes paranoia. The conclusion, "*Everyone* is pushing me!" implies as a logical response to be suspicious of everyone.

When our feeling misrepresents social reality, we act inappropriately. If fear tells us we are under attack when we are only being guided, we flee the thing we need. Feelings may jerk us about as their narrow take engulfs us.

As we edge into this domain with students, the most familiar arrow in our quiver is our premier instructional technique—*urging them to do what we want*. In the affective sphere, however, this has limited value. While most instruction elicits behavior they can carry out regardless of how they feel, their feeling itself is not so accessible. Also, as long as we tell them what to think, feel, and do, the motive for their action lies outside them. It affects them only to the extent of our influence on them. We want them instead to practice bringing their emotions into awareness, understand the appropriate action they imply, and eventually do this reliably on their own.

Direct awareness of a feeling is the primary entryway, but with feelings, as with many things, we can guide them only up to the level of detail we can distinguish. If you want a bullet to go 2,200 feet per second, you distinguish its velocity from 2,100 feet per second in order to bring criterion details under control. Managing feelings depends similarly on distinguishing them accurately.

They are irregular first because children are not alert even to the zone where management occurs. Sensations appear to them to arise randomly, and they do not recognize how to do much about them. In presenting ways to guide them, we assert that children 1) can notice what occurs within, 2) give it meaning, and 3) exert choices over it. The direction of management is to recognize its message but apply broader comprehension.

Next we look at generating good feelings.

SUMMARY

1. We need to educate children regardless of their condition when they reach us.
2. The two best predictors of adult maladjustment are poor peer relations in the first three grades and antisocial behavior in the second three grades.
3. Students receiving systematic affective learning score significantly better academically.
4. Values are bleached out when students feel alone and invisible.
5. Feelings aid growth and affect behavior.
6. Students need to be able to "plug in" to the teacher as a stable emotional resource.
7. Anger is an attempt to increase our own power and signals poor relations with students.

8. When conditions elicit your anger or frustration, aim at problem solving with fascination.

9. Our sense of safety influences the significance of the material we can address voluntarily.

10. Positive or negative teacher beliefs tend to separate good and poor teachers.

11. Students are more likely to learn in depth as their feelings are positive.

12. Students' feelings of safety are a precondition for important things they learn.

13. Students' feelings are a signal driving them toward certain behaviors.

NOTES

1. "Home Learning Experiences Boost Low-Income Kids' School Readiness," *Sciencedaily.com*, June 17, 2011, describes a study in the journal *Child Development*, June 17, 2011, about 1,850 children and the influence of their mothers' engagement with their learning. "Home Learning Experiences Boost Low-Income Kids' School Readiness." (*ScienceDaily*. Retrieved June 25, 2011, from http://www.sciencedaily.com/releases/2011/06/110617081538.htm). Also, Patrick Welsh, "The Key to a Good Education: Parents," *USA Today*, June 21, 2011. Welsh, a senior high English teacher, draws from his own experience but presents his view as refuting an attack on teachers for not educating everyone up to the bar set by the best performing students. Expectations on teachers can indeed be unreasonable, but a reasonable one on the system concerns allocation of resources before students even arrive. The system is responsible for educating them as they are when they step into school and it should assign resources accordingly.

2. L. Kohlberg, J. LaCross, and D. Ricks, "The Predictability of Adult Mental Health from Childhood Behavior," in B. B. Wolman (Ed.), *Manual of Child Psychopathology* (pp. 1217–1284) (New York: McGraw-Hill, 1972).

3. Should anyone retain the illusion that we handle these problems adequately, a current longitudinal study suggests otherwise. Claudio Sanchez, "Texas Schools Study: Most Kids Have Been Suspended," *National Public Radio*, July 19, 2011, www.npr.org/2011/07/19/138495061/report-details-texas-school-disciplinary-policies. A study titled Breaking Schools' Rules followed a million Texas seventh graders for six years. During those years, 60 percent were expelled or suspended, 15 percent were repeat offenders 11 times or more, minority kids were punished disproportionately, and students involved were more likely to repeat a grade, not graduate, or have further problems.

4. Sarah D. Sparks, "Study Finds Social-Skills Teaching Boosts Academics," *Education Week* (Online), February 4, 2011. Sparks's article summarizes the report in *Child Development*, February 4, 2011, on the work of University of Chicago professor emeritus Joseph Durlak and others.

5. Daniel Goleman, *Emotional Intelligence: Why It Can Matter More Than IQ* (New York, Bantam Dell, 1995). A good summary of how the brain is designed to combine thought and emotion in our perceptions, understanding, and actions, and the importance of managing emotions.

6. David Brooks, *The Social Animal: The Hidden Sources of Love, Character, and Achievement* (New York: Random House, 2011). Emotions, Brooks explains, are at the foundation of reason, and central to how we believe and value the world. In a TV

interview, he summarized many of his findings with the comment, "We learn from people we love." With the principle rarely spoken aloud in schools yet voiced here by a conservative political commentator, it reflects mainstream social experience.

7. "The Perceptual Organization of Effective Teachers," Florida Studies in the Helping Professions, No. 37. In Arthur W. Combs et al., "Social Sciences" (Gainesville: University of Florida, 1969), available at www.eric.ed.gov.

FOUR

Practice Good Feelings

Methods for generating good feelings

In a classroom setting, how do you teach children to manage their feelings and attitudes? To get better at anything, they practice it. To get better at eliciting good feelings, they practice it. While voluminous program materials are available, the methods below presume only a teacher guiding student activity.

Most of the methods can be adapted for any age, but for initial ease of use they fall into three categories. *All ages:* Consult, Opening a Day, Competence with Feelings, Tracking an Idea. *Younger students:* Appreciation Time, Listing Positive Behavior, Two Lines, Basic Recall. *Upper elementary to high school:* Total Attention, Correcting Thoughts, and Impulse Control.

CONSULT

A Consult (accent first syllable) creates rapid awareness of the feeling-related impact of events and increases students' affective vocabulary. Feelings typically are embedded in experiences that can be described and then the feeling component recognized. In a Consult, we ask a question about a group experience like, "What did you feel when that occurred?" or "What was the first thought that came to your mind?" Everyone answers in turn with a single word or phrase.[1]

Why use it? Brian in meltdown is not the only one affected. Some may have been frightened by it; others brought to the edge of tears, offended, or annoyed. Open expression of others' reactions conveys to the child the impact of his actions. His crying may generate feelings of sympathy or concern and alert you to a tack you may wish to take. Your fresh perception of the needs of both the class and Brian guide you in what to do.

You say, for instance, "Let's talk about what just happened. I'm going to ask a question. Think of your own answer for it, and then we'll go around quickly and hear everyone's answer. Here's the question: 'What did you feel when Brian was crying?'"

The question contains no judgment of Brian but is factual and does not steer students toward a preferred response. Brian is about to hear his connection to everyone. From peers who possess a vocabulary for emotions, he might hear sad, afraid, sympathetic, startled, disgusted, anxious, uneasy, worried, or interested. Their words reflect the impact on them of crying itself and their bond with Brian. He is immersed in significant material.

Hearing a feeling named, you can then examine the thought behind it: "What made you sad about it?" "What made you angry?" "What worried you?" At first children's answers are sketchy. As you pose the question, *they practice assigning words to their personal reaction, words socially relevant by their origin in a common experience.* Then together you resolve the problem presented.

You can do this with positive experiences also. Perhaps a special class event is announced. You ask, "What was your first feeling or thought when you heard?" As you tease out their answer in a word or phrase, they practice noticing and describing their inner state and broaden their self-awareness.

A stream of significant events is likely in any school year: a student's outburst, someone's tragedy, a family moving away, a happy event in one's life, a conflict, frustration over an equipment malfunction, disappointment over losing a possession, a dispute over sharing, who should get credit for something, and interpretations of an event that need to be talked out.

Two students arguing over being first in line to enter the classroom in the morning offers learning: "So class, what was your first thought when Akim and Jose argued about their place in line? Let's hear from everyone." The method helps stretch children's perceptions to a larger frame of reference.

When students realize they have a valid response to what occurs around them, they are more open to teachable moments. School may be the only place they are encouraged actually to think about what they will do and why. They need to notice that their own effort is worth it and that it achieves success. They judge the first from the feelings they experience and the second from how others respond. When anything unexpected happens, reflect on what the class might glean from it or ask students outright, "What can we learn from that?" Hear quickly from everyone who has an opinion.

By pointing their attention toward cause and effect in the feeling sector, we convey that 1) we value self-awareness, 2) we respect each one's personal feeling, 3) people can feel differently about the same thing and the same about different things, 4) there are many ways to manage feelings, and 5) they can safely talk about them.

OPENING A DAY

Introduced to an assembly of elementary students as one who could help them with their feelings and relationships, a counselor asks, "How many of you were unhappy sometime in the past week?"

When about 80 percent raise their hand, he exclaims, "Great! We have lots of customers!"

In truth, of course, unhappy feelings work against us. We are startled when a student throws a chair or bursts into tears or bullies another, but even short of these overt actions, their feelings operate constantly. If one of your challenges is children not cooperating, typically a feeling drives them. That they "don't listen to reason" means they listen to something else, usually their dominant feeling. Managing the feeling differs from ordering their behavior: acknowledge its presence, understand its meaning, and choose a constructive way to handle or express it.

Opening a Day is a good time to set them on this track. You might have a check-in for eight minutes that students can count on. You would say, "Would you all just look inside and notice what your feeling is?" You pause, check your own, say an honest sentence about it, and then do a Consult: "Let's go around and hear their feeling from everyone." The question lets them know we want to treat them kindly and that they are safe putting words to what they feel.

It goes without saying that if we scream at them fifteen minutes later or tolerate this from them, we mock our message. Whatever our words *say* to reassure them, they truly are not safe around us. Their first issue is emotional safety, which they grasp from the respect we give their self-expression.

Starting the day with older students wary of attracting judgments or putdowns, you might add, "If you don't know or prefer not to comment, just say 'pass.'" Today a student may be emotionally neutral, but his answer alerts you to connect quietly with him later. If many answer that way or some do it consistently, *they regard the climate in the room as unsafe.* As you use alternate means to change their attitudes, more gain confidence that they can reveal their feeling, and the number of passes will decline.

Having heard what everyone is feeling, you can pick one and say, "Let's talk briefly about how that feeling might come up and how someone might handle it." Hear their thoughts for a few minutes, conclude with a one-sentence take-home summary, and turn to the day's material. Such time helps decompress distractive feelings and make the remaining time more efficient.

To one teacher doing a morning check-in, a student answered "sad." The teacher heard answers from the other twenty-five in the room, returned to the student, and asked what made him sad.

"My aunt died last night," the student said quietly. Gasps and tears erupted from the class, many of whom had known his aunt. The teacher expressed sympathy and regret, and then conducted almost an hour-long discussion of losses others had faced. This event brought them together emotionally and appeared later to have been a watershed for altering some severe dysfunctions.

COMPETENCE WITH FEELINGS

Once a week you might name a feeling (e.g., by assigning a rotating selection committee) and engage the class in discussing it. The following stimulate thinking:

- Give the dictionary meaning of the feeling.
- In what settings or situations is it likely to occur?
- What experiences has anyone had with it or observed in others?
- What triggers or sets it off?
- What are ways to handle or express it? What choices are open?
- What are the outcomes of the different choices?
- What plan do you want to make now about handling the feeling?

Beginning list: afraid, alone, annoyed, belonging, cheerful, close, confused, down, excited, embarrassed, guilty, curious, free, friendly, good, grumpy, happy, hopeful, hurt, jealous, joyful, left out, lonely, loved, loving, mad, proud, sad, scared, shy, silly, surprised, worried. If students use the word "bad" to describe their feeling, steer them toward a more specific word.

Expanded list: adequate, affectionate, alert, ambitious, angry, apathetic, apologetic, anxious, assured, awed, awkward, appreciated, bored, competent, concerned, contented, controlling, dependent, depressed, desire for attention, determined, disappointed, distant, ecstatic, edgy, empty, energetic, enthusiastic, envious, flowing, focused, frustrated, gratitude, grief, hassled, hate, helpless, inadequate, independent, indignant, inferior, insecure, involved, irritated, jealous, lost, masterful, mistrusting, needed, neglected, neutral, noninvolved, nostalgic, optimistic, pessimistic, possessive, powerful, protective, put down, rebellious, regretful, rejected, rejecting, relaxed, relieved, remorse, resentful, respectful, responsible, secure, self-blame, self-conscious, serene, shame, small, sorry for self, spaced out, stressed, stubborn, superior, temper, threatened, tired, tolerant, tranquil, troubled, trusting, uneasy, unneeded, unwanted, valuable, wanted, weak, weary, willful, wondering, worthless, wronged.

Discuss the selected feeling objectively. The result you want is their practice *arousing desired feelings and diminishing unwanted ones by choice*. To start them off at this, perhaps the simplest intervention is to ask them to try to slow down a feeling just by choosing to. Can they reduce an unpleasant one or increase a positive one by 10 percent?

In exerting even such a small degree of control, they engage the key attitude of managing their feeling, and often discover that they can rapidly improve at it. It reassures them to know that a feeling does not define them and that they are not helpless in the face of it.

TRACK AN IDEA

Imagine that you encounter an important idea that could help students manage their world. It enables them to understand their experience in a different way, and you would like to get it across. A time-efficient approach is: *Present it briefly. On following days spend just a consistent minute or two to inquire about their application or perception of it.* Once recognizing its relevance, they only need an opportunity to express themselves about it. In a few days of checking the idea, they begin watching for it all day. You might wrap it around an objective fact or statistic like the following:

> How many of you expect to get married someday? Have friends all your life? A researcher named John Gottman looked into a thousand marriages to try to tell which ones were going to break up and which stayed together. What he found probably applies the same to friendships. He found that the marriages most likely to stay together were different from those that split up in their number of "going toward" versus "going away" behaviors toward each other. A "going toward" action is praise, help, appreciation, support—positive actions of all kinds. A "going away" is criticism, blame, unkindness, being inconsiderate, lying, and the like. Strong marriages had *five times more going toward than going away* actions, and the strongest ones had up to 30 to 1 toward versus away actions.[2]

Once they get the idea, daily take just a minute or two to nudge their assimilation of it with questions like these:

- Who noticed a going toward action today? Think about a time you were with a friend. How many going toward actions did you do? Let's hear a number from everyone.
- Why do you think anyone would *choose* to give a going away response to anyone?
- Do you give more going toward actions to some people than to others? How does that affect your relationships?

- If you wanted more friends, what going toward actions could you do more of?

Present scenarios where the toward/away distinction is not clear and challenge them to figure it out. For example, if you disagree with a friend, what makes it going toward or away? Help them examine the impact of the action, intent, and perceptions. In time, touch on relationship issues, communication skills, and life principles. If they can look forward to a discussion of it, they will keep a relevant issue in mind all day.

APPRECIATION TIME

Appreciation Time *helps cause a good feeling by asking them to look for one.* A standing need accounts for its success. Students are pervasively uncertain about how others regard them. They wonder if they are liked, disliked, important, unimportant, close, distant—what? Even on good days they may be painfully self-conscious about their appearance, sensitive to how others take their comments, presume criticism where none was intended, and hate the prospect of being put down. What adult cannot recall a childhood discount that stung deeply? We want to plant them upon their strengths by asking them to do a simple thing.

Many years ago, researchers studying playground behavior of kindergartners counted their median aggressive acts at forty-two per day. They then instituted a ten-minute daily sharing time, asking students, "Who was friendly to you today?" and allowed those named to take a happy-face badge from the wall. Incidents quickly dropped to a median of nine.

They changed the question to "Who was unfriendly to you today?" and the median aggressive acts climbed back to forty per day. When they changed the question a final time back to "Who was friendly to you today?" incidents dropped this time to six. The essence of the change was that "friendliness became the way to gain recognition."[3]

The report brought to mind working with adult groups. Being acknowledged for something positive gives people a green light to do it more, hinting that some adaptation of the method should work with all ages. Noticer and noticed are both reinforced when one recognizes another's positive behavior. The first feels competent and benevolent, and the second appreciated.

To apply the method, use terms that fit your students, such as "friendly," "gave you good feelings," "helped you feel good," or "did something nice for you." Invite each to take a turn but without pressing anyone. Introduce the plan:

> Every day at this time, I'm going to ask you a question and let everyone give their answer. The question is, "Can you name someone who has given you a good feeling and tell what they did?" Let's go around the

class now. Gena, who gave you a good feeling? How did they do that? Thank you. Aaron, who gave you a good feeling? How did they do that?

Most primary grade children are ready with a flood of acknowledgements of other's actions. If at first only a couple respond, continue to offer the question and you will focus them.

Starting about in second grade, some children believe that no one intends good feelings toward them, and they need the exercise even more. Gena may be unaware of others' friendly actions and unable to imagine herself receiving them. The question teaches her that the issue is significant, that she will have an answer eventually, and her answer will be right. She is the sole authority on what she feels. She consults herself rather than guess what the teacher wants.

The exercise works best done at the same time every day so the class becomes accustomed to it, preferably after free time such as a game, recess, or lunch. It enhances sharing if they are already alert and talkative.

In a large classroom of fourth graders who a few weeks before had been violent, hateful, and uncooperative, the teacher spent forty-five minutes after lunch one day going around the room. First he asked each one individually, "Would you *name* someone who gave you a good feeling?" After they answered one at a time, he went around again with "And what did they *do* that gave you the good feeling?" They had played a team game during lunch and had many good feelings to share. Their rapt attention to each other made it clear that the activity met a pervasive need.

You can defer your own report to use at your discretion. Your personal feeling has different significance than your role-based behavior. It may already be within your repertoire to say privately, "Zach, when you helped Rachel, it touched me. It made me happy. Good going!" Your tone of voice and genuine feeling inform Zach that his action reached you as a person, and you may be able to envision you and your class together sharing the positive impact of experiences.

A legitimate question arises, however, over injecting your own feelings. People usually appreciate leaders who exhibit them, are enthusiastic, and know where they are going. Teachers can become master encouragers, habitually notice the next step, and nudge students to take it, but even this can be overused. It can limit students just when we want them instead to tap their own resources and independently discover a personal answer.

Success with Appreciation Time arises from their self-awareness, not from our direction. We "toss the ball" to them and let them devise their own response. We want the meaning of the question to appeal to them rather than our coaxing.

Another caution is students' desire for control over their thoughts. The more overtly we try to change their thinking, the more easily they deflect it. Information they accept automatically penetrates most deeply, which is the premise of advertising. Teachers remain unobtrusive *by using minimal but frequent means to acknowledge students' positive actions.*

A glance, meeting their eye, and a wink may say everything needed. A nod and hint of a smile lets the student know that we noticed his action and valued it, particularly if we have already opened a train of thought with him, checked his assimilation of it, and now just catch his eye as he acts upon it. In a second, he realizes, "I tried it and it turned out well." We avoid overcoaching their responses.

If we believe it is needed, we can prepare the ground by drawing on cooperative students. Tell a couple ahead of time the question you will ask, and invite them to think of comments they could offer. If you notice events on the playground or in the classroom that generate good feelings (one passes the ball to another, they take turns, they share, they help another, etc.), you can ask them how they felt during those moments. A peer demonstrating a new behavior can help others adopt it.

Ultimately the activity must generate its own energy. We pose the question, ask it of each student in turn, mentally step back, and trust it to engage him or her. Grappling with it, the students look inward where their identity governs and an authentic response awaits. Tomorrow they may find an answer they take as their own, and their interest sustains the experience.

With pre-kindergarten children, a *secret friend* approach may fit periodically. The younger students are, the more completely they are consumed by their own perspective but eventually notice others' actions apart from their own. Immediately before a recess, lunch, or other free time, speak to each one personally and assign them a secret friend, another student in their class.

They reveal their secret friend only afterward, when the teacher brings them all together and they listen to each one in turn. The teacher invites them to tell how their secret friend was friendly, helpful, or considerate *to anyone*. If they volunteer how they themselves did these things, you accept their answer, nod, smile, and repeat your question about noticing others.

TEACHER QUESTIONS

Questions about Appreciation Time may apply also to broader concerns about addressing children's feelings:

"What if I'm uncomfortable answering the question myself?" You're not alone. Institutions reinforce the impersonal by reducing people and activity to their functional labels. If your role has done this to you, you and

your students may grow together as you regularly address the feeling dimension. You can learn how to admit human emotion without allowing it to rule. The direction for growth is understanding the origin of your discomfort and nudging your thought process.

Teaching styles and personalities are varied, and a focus on feelings may not come readily to some who emphasize the *work* of learning and leave students to their own moods. In such classrooms, students should know their teacher's commitment to learning and their respect for student effort. Teaching that has become emotion neutral or negative and mimics the Top Sergeant who lacks respect for them, wears students down, and can turn them against learning (cf., The Power of Teacher Beliefs in chapter 3). For you to succeed with Appreciation Time, children's good feelings need to ascend among your priorities.

"I don't think my students will want to do it." At the start, maybe not. School may have conditioned them, like you, to believe that their feelings are insignificant even though they must endure them hour by hour. But think what it means if they truly cannot recognize good feelings directed toward them. *It means they live in an emotional desert.*

Their difficulty answering doubles the importance of the question. If you are not using Appreciation Time to address this need, find another way. For children so emotionally impoverished, even small gestures make a difference: "The sound of your voice saying 'Hi' gave me a good feeling." Students need to believe that it is a good thing to acknowledge good things.

"What limitations does the method have?" It works from pre-kinder up, although older students may at first need a certain generalized acceptance of each other. Those riven by cliques, gossip, and labels may not feel safe enough even to begin. They may dismiss your early attempts and need you to address this zone with a multiprong approach.

Even a few minutes spent at it can make a difference, so time is not a problem. The method works best when students are already expressive, such as after a recess, rather than first thing in the morning when they are only half awake. And it helps at the start if they already cooperate with your leads.

"A couple students might ridicule others or sabotage it." Such behavior means they have no good feelings themselves. Some struggle with two parts inside them. One hopes for good things to happen and the other has been disappointed so often that it challenges anything purporting to be good. You might ignore their initial comments, allow time for their better side to win, and continue the exercise with those who want to make it work.

Those feeling unsafe may benefit initially from objective discussions, such as about one feeling at a time, or from other activities explained elsewhere. Once they succeed by following your instructions, applaud others' success in performing their learning, and use communication skills in a group, they slowly realize that they are safe also to intend good feelings.

"If students do cooperate with you, how does it change their behavior later?" Two aphorisms explain: *If you don't know where you're going, you'll probably end up somewhere else* and *Focus on what you want rather than on what you don't want.* The first expresses the general state of students' minds, floating this way and that, jarred by random stimuli, until a school experience points them. The younger the students, the more ephemeral their thinking and more malleable they are. We steer their behavior by offering a clear and satisfying direction for it.

Once they notice that they can direct their attention, the second aphorism guides: *Focus on what you want.* Attending to what they desire is like a homing beacon for their thinking. Unless a stronger distractive influence arises, they will think and do what they are pointed toward, following out the mental program activated in them.

You might understand this through its opposite. Imagine sending your students out for recess right after scolding them for bad behavior. Any guess what you cause? Years ago before anyone thought much about attending deliberately to students' attitudes, a fifth grade teacher watched her class at recess. When one child pushed another, she commented wryly, "I think about 75 percent of their interactions are basically cruel." A negative pattern left uninterrupted is self-reinforcing.

"Is there a danger of bad feelings coming out of this?" Bad feelings can arise unexpectedly where we look for good ones. Students may fear invasion or being focused on. Some may assume that even positive comments contain a judgment. They may be cynical about adults' inability to guide them, have stresses they want to conceal, or dismiss others' opinions.

While not causing their bad feeling, Appreciation Time may open a zone packed with them. Place yourself in their shoes and imagine feeling isolated, unappreciated, and an outsider. Then someone you regard as a stranger tells you in front of the whole world that you made him or her feel good by something you did. For a vulnerable child this could unplug tears or be dismissed as cognitively dissonant.

We should not abort the method just because unhappy feelings are possible, but only be alert to them. The benevolent stance of the class toward each is the new influence. As the class responds respectfully, a child's entire view of relationships can shift. Experiencing the activity even briefly each day, all realize they are safe and respected and that their attempts to generate good feelings in others are welcome.

LISTING POSITIVE BEHAVIOR

The younger children are, the less likely they are to know what to do with their feelings. Even if they have positive intentions, they often do not know how to express them. To stimulate their awareness, try a simple list, but with a cautionary note. So that too many visual stimuli do not disperse focus on important ideas, be sure to involve children in the meaning of any new thing you post on your classroom walls.

Brainstorm ways to be friendly. Ask students to tell you all the things they can do or have had done to them that were friendly. This provides you raw material you can use in several ways. You can make it an academic task to memorize the list perfectly, or together read it daily and invite them to add to it any items they can think of: "Passed me the ball," "Gave me a pencil," "Told me I had food on my shirt," "Tied my shoes for me." You want them aware of a score of ways to express friendship and good feelings so that they never need resort to negative behavior to meet their emotional needs.

You might start a chart with names down the side and a dozen blank columns across the top. Each day label a single new column with one friend-creating idea. Practice having them tell back all the columns so far without looking, and then a couple times a day allow them to make tallies by each other's names for behaviors they saw used. Title the chart, How I Can Be a Friend. It might list:

- Look at them
- Smile at them
- Listen to them
- Be close to them
- Include them
- Invite them
- Play with them
- Help them
- Defend them
- Watch them
- Clap for them
- Wait for them

The intent is to fix friend-making strategies so vividly in their mind that they can select and apply one instantly. In twelve days, they would be alert to a dozen helpful ideas. Challenge older students with more subtle points: "Say nice things about them to others," "Accept that they're not perfect," and "Work out disagreements with them."

Students need to know it when they do something right, so try to phrase points as an explicit behavior. Anyone watching should be able to verify their deed. Later, after they carry it out, they can more easily grasp the value involved. You point out, for example, "See? You carried out the value of *trust*." Noticing just the performance of the action before exploring its implications often suits students better. You can turn your list into a handout, give each student a copy, and work with it periodically:

1. In class, think back to a specific occasion that day such as lunch or recess when they could relate freely. Read each point on the list, and ask them to raise their hand if they remembered doing it.
2. Ask them to raise their hand if someone else did it toward them.
3. Ask them to pick someone with whom they get along well, and beside each point on the handout, rate their own behavior 0–5 on how they express it toward that student.
4. Pick someone with whom they may have a problem, friend or not, and again rate their own behavior toward that person 0–5 on each point.
5. Total up the scores they gave themselves in the two preceding tasks, and do a Consult asking for the two scores from each.
6. Discuss the meaning of one being larger than the other. What is the outcome of acting more negatively toward someone with whom they have a problem? One girl blamed others for her having few friends, but the discrepancy between her scores in steps 3 and 4 above was compelling evidence to her that she was a major cause.
7. A good use of choral repetition is having them together repeat after you: *I make friends if I treat people better.*
8. Brainstorm specific ways they could carry out each positive point. One class that was asked, "How do you welcome others?" quickly volunteered a host of ways.
9. For students who have difficulty relating to peers, confer with them privately about what happens from their attempts.
10. Discuss how they would change any of their behaviors if they wanted to make a new friend. Some they can do even distant from others. If you do not get along with certain people, you can still defend them when others criticize them behind their back and can tell what you respect about them.
11. Discuss the principle, "If you have a problem with someone, you need to treat them *better* to heal it."
12. Discuss how their friend-creating strategies have evolved and improved as they have grown older.

TWO LINES METHOD

This is a way to aid learning in kindergarten and first grade with a game-like exchange. It presumes that they listen to you and cooperate in lining up, following instructions, and taking turns. Once they understand how it works, they typically enjoy the energy and competence it draws on.

To forestall a possible objection to it, we note that some teachers protest anything smacking of unthinking repetition. An extreme example is "Blab School" in the Middle East where a teacher's sole technique is to say a sentence and the class repeats it. Our goal here is to use repetition first to teach the rules of the game so that they can then practice learning more independently. If they are just beginning to comply with a behavioral request, we start there using choral repetition of instructions.[4] We take them through steps about how to work with a partner, draw on the reinforcement of peer response, and steadily expand the content of learning they can explain on their own.

Begin by asking them to line up in two columns facing you. Name each. With colored paper on the floor, you might say, "You're the Reds," and "You're the Greens." From that point, *have each group repeat after you every step out loud just before doing it.* The first run-through may take a little more practice, but they will rapidly understand and cooperate.

Say to the Reds as though conducting an orchestra, "After me say, 'We're the Reds,'" and gesture to them to do so. Listen and watch to see that everyone complies. This absolutely safe beginning is significant because those who find it hard even to repeat a simple instruction are the ones you worry about. These have heard you ask for the behavior, they watch and listen as others do it, and now you say gently, "Conrad? Repeat after me, 'We're the Reds!' . . . Thank you." If Conrad still does not get it, you just involve him in the pattern as others carry it out.

Students readily comply with choral repetition: "Okay everyone, let's try this again and hear from everyone nice and loud. Reds, say 'We're the Reds.' Greens, say 'We're the Greens.'" So far they have put out effort, grouped themselves into teams, and were successful, noticed, and included. To help them own their learning, arrange for them to 1) learn a tiny piece and 2) say it to someone else as the answer to a question.

Ask them to turn toward the other column of students and identify the person they face who is their partner for the exercise. When you tell them, "Everyone point to your partner now," they do so willingly. If you have an odd number of students, ask the extra to join another pair: "Robert, you'll have two partners, Jenny and Aiden." You first want them to use the format smoothly before taxing their mind with learning anything. Begin with familiar knowledge.

"Reds, I want you to ask a question of the Greens. Now what are you going to do?" Pause a moment and let them think. Then lead them to the answer: "Say to me, 'We ask a question of the Greens.' So what are you going to do?" Like a choral conductor, lead them through each word as needed: "Ask . . . a question . . . of the Greens." With that, you have conveyed one rule of the game. Turn to the Greens and do the response.

"Greens, I want you to answer the question. Now, what are you going to do?"

Pause, let them think, and then lead them to the answer: "Say to me, 'Answer the question.'" You want to drive this piece home until everyone gets it and says it together. "That's right. I want you to answer the question. Now, what are you going to do? Say to me, 'We answer the question.'" Lead them through their answer, watch, and listen to everyone so that all voices chime in. Repeat each piece until you hear everyone say it correctly together.

Such thoroughness with early microsteps spells the difference between success and failure *for the students hardest to reach.* You distinguish essential details and make sure they are in place for every student, so each thinks afterward, "Well, I really nailed that!"

Repeating the words describing the upcoming step roughs in a template they can apply to any learning. You put it to work. "Reds, I want you to ask your partner, 'What is your name?' Do that, please, and Greens answer." Look at the Reds to see if everyone can do it.

If there are stragglers, repeat: "Let's do it again. Reds, I want you to ask your partner, 'What is your name?' Do that please." Then turn to the Greens and do the same thing back to the Reds. "Greens, I want you to ask your partner, 'What is your name?' Do that please, and Reds answer."

Once understood, this pattern works with any knowledge you can phrase as question and answer. Each side repeats after you the correct wording of the question and answer. You install the plan for the current micropiece expressed in Q and A *together as a class* before you ask them to carry it out *individually* with their partner, assuring them that they can succeed in learning anything. 1) Deliver a piece of learning, 2) specify it as a question and answer, 3) allow everyone to repeat each part perfectly after you, and 4) demonstrate it to a peer as Q and A, meshing conscious learning with social needs.

What content do you use? The most important at first are simple behavioral plans. Understand the problem. Children must figure out their approach to the world as they move about on their own. Toddlers try things out and rapidly develop a personal style. By the time we meet them at school years later, they have already settled into habits. A parent declares that her child having rough going in kindergarten was "that way" at one year old!

Some of their strategies are adaptive, others tentative, and others explicitly counterproductive. By giving them constructive options, we expand their versatility. We can plug into the Two Lines method anything we want them to learn and might start with behaviors that help a classroom hum:

- What do you do when someone falls down? *Help them up.*
- What do you do when someone loses something? *Help them find it.*
- What do you do when you make a mess? *Clean it up.*
- What do you do when you want someone to help you? *Say "Please."*
- What do you do when someone helps you? *Say "Thank you."*
- What do you do when someone thanks you? *Say "You're welcome,"*
- What do you do when you want someone to play with you? *Invite them.*

- What do you do when someone talks to you? *Listen to them.*
- What do you do when someone needs something? *Help them find it.*
- What do you do when someone is hurt? *Ask them how you can help.*
- What do you do when you hurt someone's feelings? *Say, "I'm sorry."*

It expands their social skills to partner them eventually with everyone else in the class (cf., *Teaching Students to Work Harder and Enjoy It: Practice Makes Permanent,* chapter 7, section "The Bracelet Aid" for an easy way to do this). They need confidence that they can practice with anyone. Make sure they learn a part well by repeating it together after you, guaranteeing their success when you ask them to demonstrate it alone to their partner.

You can easily deepen their sense of success by returning often to previously mastered learning. Think of its demonstration like a runner doing a victory lap or a baseball home run hitter circling the bases. The hard part is done and we can afford a few seconds to let them enjoy the expression of it while simultaneously deepening it. With the Two Lines method, you can work briskly through an array of easy details, sharpening their sense of teamwork and encouraging their confidence in their knowledge:

- What number comes after 19? *Twenty!*
- What letter comes after P? *Q!*
- How do you spell *cat*? *C-A-T!*
- What color is a banana? *Yellow!*
- What animal has a trunk? *Elephant!*

BASIC RECALL

A visitor may experience a tug on the heart seeing a kindergartner wandering about the classroom in his own lonely bubble while the teacher keeps everything going with a couple dozen others. Isolation, typically accompanied by poor listening habits, can be found at any level. Since there is "not enough teacher to go around," the only alternative is to *take the time to train children to meet each other's needs.* We can arrange for them to practice the attention that brings an isolated student into connection with others.

At a primitive level, we first attend to another's words enough to recall them. You meet your friend Bill, ask what he did over the weekend, he says he went for a hike, and later you mention to your family that Bill went hiking. Adults do this automatically, filing what they hear according to a reason for recalling it.

Children do this less than we would like with schoolwork because they hear a stream of sound not differentiated by importance. Why should they interrupt their interesting thoughts to remember a detail from the stream? Nothing innate to them or intrinsic to the material shouts at them, "And be sure to remember this!" Because they can count on the teacher driving it home later if it deserves recall, *they know they can dismiss anything the teacher does not demand,* leaving them with only a sporadic intent to listen.

We can alter this fairly easily, even with the very young. We set them up to practice remembering one thing they themselves select.

A first grade teacher assigned three sets of partners and three topics (pets, food, and games) for three rounds. In limited classroom space they sat on the floor elbow to elbow. In each round, the speaker talked for one minute on the topic, the listener told back one thing they remembered, and they switched roles. The teacher told the listener in each pair, "Zipper your lip" so they would not interrupt, and they did this with dramatic gestures.

"Just look at the person talking," she said. "Don't interrupt, and remember one thing they say." She kept time carefully, changed partners and topics for each round, and the whole thing was over in ten minutes.

A different teacher conducted the class the next day and later asked the regular teacher, "What have you been doing with these children? They're paying attention better than ever!" Hot weather had begun and the children were generally more squirrelly, but a single ten-minute experience changed their behavior noticeably.

Your class may not need such an exercise if they already listen carefully and remember what others say. If you decide to try it, you might first teach them the method before you apply it. Split your problem. First *they just grasp the rules,* removing all doubt in their minds about what they will do. Convey the plan before executing it.

"Class, tomorrow we will have a special experience but first we need to make sure everyone understands it. There are three steps: 'Look at the speaker, don't interrupt, and tell back one thing the speaker says.'" Ask them to repeat the steps and at random moments through the day, ask "Who can tell the three steps for tomorrow?" Applaud their answers.

We tend to skip such preparation because we assume we can start anything and steer it as we go, but working independently even for a minute, students follow the plan as it rests on their mind. As they tell the rules back and forth to each other the day before, it instructs their subconscious that they will all do this as the rules say, and their social bonds reinforce it. Clear group norms bring allies to your side. One child points to another and tells you indignantly, "He isn't following the rules!" A deeper metapurpose is your intent to teach them *how to form a mental plan and carry it out.* For you, these are the guidelines:

1. Choose three age-appropriate topics.
2. Select three sets of partner pairs.

3. Set a time for the rounds.
4. Run three rounds with different partners and topics.
5. Within each round, partner pairs switch roles.
6. Have students master the rules before running the experience.

The students learn these rules before starting:

1. Look at the speaker.
2. Do not interrupt.
3. Tell back one thing the speaker says.

Like any group activity, this one can be sabotaged. Because you work with details—partners, topics, minutes, rounds—any change of focus can occasion a problem. Be clear with the sequence yourself. If you arrive with partner pairs and topics already selected, you shortcut distractions and disagreements that could occur. If distracted, you may easily forget to have them switch roles in the same pair or forget to tell back one thing at the end of each half-round. Smooth out the flow in your mind so you get a feel for the efficiency that makes it work:

> Here are your partners. Please find your partner and face each other. (Get them positioned properly, and instruct them which of their pair speaks first.) Speakers, the topic is . . . Listeners, look at the speaker, don't interrupt, and remember one thing they say. Please begin. . . . Please end. Listeners tell one thing the speaker said. . . . Okay, same partners, same topic, but switch roles. (Repeat the same pattern.) Here are your partners for the second round. . . . (Run the pattern three times with different partners and topics.)

Repeating the experience periodically, you might invite them to brainstorm topics they can talk about, and set longer times for each round for older students (cf., *Effective Classroom Turnaround: Practice Makes Permanent*, appendix, for lists of age-grouped topics).

TOTAL ATTENTION

Much student talk is a surface response to the moment. For deeper thinking, we need to set up conditions that encourage it, beginning just with recalling what another said. Having done that and wishing to reply, we then choose whether or not to dig deeper into our own thoughts. A powerful condition influencing that choice *is the degree of attention we receive from the other*, a skill we can help students develop.

We offer them a lifetime gift when we enable them to listen exhaustively to each other. Both speaker and listener benefit. The latter understands the other better while the former develops his/her own thinking. When another listens, we expect to make sense to them, but thinking quietly, we easily mix up images, half-formed phrases, and fragments of perception. In explaining, we give sequence and order to the pieces.

Those weighing on us most are usually colored by burdensome emotions and leave us vulnerable. We noted earlier how a feeling of safety assures us that we can wade into this sensitive material. If we can help students generate safety in each other, we enable them to head off problems while they are small, resolve disagreements before they are blown out of proportion, and organize their thinking more soundly. Left unsafe, they are confined inside superficial thoughts and involuntary reactions.

Especially during middle and high school when peer opinions have such an impact, students rarely encounter a setting in which they can explore their thinking safely unless they are in so much trouble their parents spring for professional counseling. Even *possible* negative judgment can halt them. Many schools, with their emphasis on physical security, fail to address why students still remain emotionally unsafe.

The dominant reason is that teachers judge students and students judge each other. Think about it. A judgment is like a spear hurled at a chink in another's armor. By deliberately directing critical thoughts at someone, *we intend* to strike their vulnerability. We say deliberately, "There's something wrong with you," which even unspoken constitutes a threat.

In contrast, imagine a new student's relief after his first week at your school when he realizes that *no one here criticizes anyone! Everyone looks for the best in each other!* Imagine multiplying that feeling, and the confidence it would give him to open up what bothers him.

In sum, to convey the safety that allows constructive thought to emerge, *suspend negative judgment and criticism.* Reassure others that we do not threaten them, that they are accepted as they are.

Several aspects of our general approach increase safety. Appreciation Time and other ways of exploring feelings respectfully tell everyone, "We're looking for the good in you, not the flaws." Safety increases also as they practice remembering what others say at the basic level. They mix and match ideas in conversation and become comfortable expressing their thoughts to peers in group discussion.

Signs of readiness for the next step are 1) class leaders actively discourage gossip, 2) the social atmosphere is consistently positive and supportive, 3) students spontaneously applaud each other's efforts, and 4) the group makes a conscious choice never to embarrass or hurt another.[5]

Inside that umbrella of safety, we arrange adequate time. A parallel is a conversation with a stranger on an airplane. Time moves slowly, interruptions are minimal, and because this person is not in your life, they are neutral to your ideas. They cannot use the information against you, so you can afford to bring up what otherwise you might not mention. The key condition remaining is *for listeners to give speakers their entire attention without diverting into their own associations with what is said.*

The issue of distraction is central. Think of it this way. Typically if one talks about going to the beach, others call up their own trips to the beach, a comparison of beaches ensues, and they segue to associated ideas. For the first speaker, however, the point of the trip to the beach may have been a relationship that concerned him, how to connect with the person he accompanied. The thoughts significant to him may have been so fragile that he could develop them *only if others refrained from interfering with them*.

To set up the relatively rare conditions enabling speakers to explore these fragile margins of their thinking, we ask listeners to look at the speaker, follow *their* train of thought, and build in their own mind *only* a narrative of the speaker's words. Two verbal responses are welcome from the listener: 1) to praise or admire anything said and 2) at the end to summarize the speaker's words comprehensively if they feel it appropriate.

A helpful form for the latter step is for the listener to draw together the speaker's ideas so accurately that the speaker himself could have said them, entering perfectly into his thought-stream: "So I, Jake, had this happen . . . and I thought . . . and I felt . . . etc."[6]

To introduce the activity, discuss first how they can be safe for each other, help them select among issues they may wish to talk about, and then set up the experience:

> Please find a partner for this exercise, someone you feel comfortable talking to. . . . Face each other and sit close enough that you can hear each other easily. Let's start with twenty minutes per person. Choose who speaks first and who listens. . . . In fifteen minutes I'll call time and ask listeners to take a couple minutes to summarize to the speaker what they said. Speakers talk about anything you want to. You might start with your personal experiences, think out loud about school, issues that interest you, anything that challenges you, or just about life and the world.
>
> Listeners give the speaker full eye contact. Think about what they say and form in your mind just the picture they talk about. Lay aside your own thoughts that spring up, and keep your attention just on the speaker. When they pause, wait for them to continue, or mention anything they say that draws your respect, admiration, or appreciation. The last step for each round is *the speaker tells the listener* anything the listener did that helped the speaker develop his/her ideas. It helps listeners to know that the quality of their attention made a difference. Whatever is said is between you and your partner and is not to be shared with others. Everyone's personal thoughts are their own.

Students benefit significantly from a half hour weekly—an hour divided with a partner—to integrate seven days worth of experience, feelings, and learning, but many do not get that much in a year. Adults presume students have no perceptions, thoughts, or feelings worth patiently stringing together and then are puzzled why they appear so limited in thinking or wrong-headed in behavior. Safe, sustained, thoughtful attention from another is a powerful curative for what ails most children.

IMPULSE CONTROL

Maturity enables us temporarily to assume an alternate point of view, see something as others see it, or consider a problem along its timeline. If we could always remember, "How will this turn out in the end?" we would avoid many a debacle. To lead students' thinking this way, we can plot it along stages of progress. We begin with the least useful in the series and help them work up to the most useful. As a class activity, we discuss each step and encourage students to watch for it in their experience.

An impersonal beginning is with news of local crimes, police reports, and altercations. Speculate together on how impulses might have affected people's actions and the foresight they employed. You might set up a discussion this way:

1. Explain that you will present six stages marking their degree of control of their actions.
2. Invite them to apply the stages to events from their life or with people they know where an impulse to act inappropriately was at stake. It may have been resisted, or followed out leading to loss afterward.
3. Assure them that you will not ask them to tell the class the event they select if they would rather not, but only notice where it stands among the stages discussed.
4. As you explain each stage, involve students in connecting it to the events they select and in the news stories you present.

Stage 1. Loss. A teacher may be puzzled that a student admits unacceptable behavior yet continues it. The teacher reinstructs, the student agrees, but the behavior persists. A way to understand this is that the teacher mandate alights in his brain distant from the niche driving the behavior. Few neurons tie the one reading "I'm going to do this" to the one saying "The teacher wants me to do X instead."[7] Later the teacher may loom large, but in the moment, the student forgets. The larger picture returns only as delayed outcomes impact him.

His final experience of loss or injury is the most remote beginning for change. Many young people fail to appreciate the quality of their actions. They may need to face the principal for misbehaving or go to jail briefly for theft or violence and later acknowledge that "just being arrested turned me around." Those with an undeveloped emotional nature may not even feel loss from their misbehavior but await consequences to deliver the message.

You might say to your students, "Remember your feelings after the experience when it came home to you that you lost something from it. All you can do at this stage is just let it hit you. Summarize in your mind what the effect was."

Stage 2. Regret. This stage still occurs well after the fact, but the person realizes he did wrong and regrets it for that reason—a step beyond just avoiding trouble. The unpleasant feeling is strong enough that he realizes he does not want to act that way anymore. He may notice that another is genuinely hurt, a friend is injured, or a possession ruined, and he made it happen. The effect of his action matters to him apart from his own loss.

Say, "A step up is realizing that others lost something too. They may have been hurt or let down, and you regret the effect it had apart from your own loss."

Stage 3. Correction. The student realizes immediately after the event that it was the wrong thing to do and sets about correcting it. He sees how he made others or himself unhappy, broke rules, or let down expectations and redirects actions still open to him. Items are repaired, messes cleaned up, obligations accepted and met, apologies made. The note beyond the earlier stages is his active response.

Say, "Right after you've done something, you realize you should not have, and you try to change what you do next. You try to set things right."

Stage 4. Self-guidance. As internality increases, the student observes the thoughts guiding him in the midst of his actions: "Here I am arguing with my friends. I'm upset and I don't need to do this." As he notices that he is blaming, gossiping, breaking rules, or stealing, he steers his way out. He recognizes how he can choose better and does so at once.

Say, "In this step you notice your attitude and take hold of it even while it drives your actions. Before, you waited to see the outer effects of your behavior, but now you understand how you set them in motion inside you and you want to change them right away."

Stage 5. Foresight. He foresees how to guide behavior before it occurs and avoids negative consequences in the first place. He tells his friends, "I can't do that. My father would kill me if he found out," proposing a reason his friends can understand. For himself, he realizes the wrong, steers away from it, and channels the experience toward a better outcome. The situation, his prior inner experiences, and his understanding come together in a self-aware moment when reasons confront impulses and win. The values he chooses begin to govern his early choices.

Say, "Because you're alert to how your thinking and feelings set you up, you increasingly see ahead what will happen and decide not even to go there."

Stage 6. Habit. Consistent foresight returns students easily to the constructive option, and events work out better. Their impulses are seldom tested because habits steer them away. Say, "The final stage is having habits of thought so positive and clear to you that you seldom encounter a problem. You avoid trouble before it happens."

To help them apply the stages personally, have each make up a check sheet. Turn a piece of paper sideways. Write the six categories down the left side and, to the right across the top, the seven days of the week. Twice a week—often enough that they can still remember what occurred—have them think about each category since they last did this and give themselves tallies under the appropriate day for any stage they experienced. Periodically discuss their collective findings. You might also have them learn the list by heart so they check themselves more easily. Recognizing a single step as it occurs reminds them of the set.

CORRECTING THOUGHTS

Bullying is just one deficit in social/emotional self-management. That it has become a national problem signals how poorly we have addressed the larger issue of guiding thoughts and feelings. If children had not died from it, bullying probably would have remained below the national radar as just another thing kids do.

All our actions emerge from a thought stream. To change an outcome, we change the stream. We insert a redirect order at the right spot, like a farmer diverting a brook at the best point to irrigate his fields, changing the step that makes the most difference. Typically, A goes to B and then to C. Corrected, A goes to B and then by choice jumps past C to land at D.

Most who want to change their thinking just identify a new thought, hope they will remember it when they need it, and are chagrined when the moment comes and they blow it. We try instead to help them foresee *when* to call on a new thought, *identify* the thought it will replace, and make the substitution beforehand. They might decide, "When I meet Adam, instead of the usual complaining we do, I'll think of something positive to say."

We might assume that changing our thinking would be impossibly difficult, but it is easier than one would expect. Our mainstream thoughts seem to bump against a natural upper limit of between eight and fifteen, with the median about a dozen. Ninety percent of our thinking may recycle a scant handful of ideas. The reason appears to be that we organize our attention around our primary emotions and our brain can only accommodate a few. Only so many elephants fit into a living room.

We tend to elicit a characteristic emotion for each part of our day, like "This is wearing me down" or "This is interesting." Recurring feelings spur recurring thoughts. If the feeling is negative, the thought usually is too, and they reinforce each other in a dance that may last for years. Perhaps you recall a single idea preoccupying you this week.

The upside to the limited range of our thoughts is that changing only a few can make a big difference. It has been suggested that most people's problems come down to a decision whether to use Plan A or Plan B. Big changes are seldom complicated but usually recast only a few items in our life. Altering even one may affect everything.

To correct our thinking, we identify habitual thoughts, separate out the negative ones, and change them to positives that enable us to handle the same situation better. Recoding an event allows us to emphasize a novel angle—an issue's importance, an invitation to mastery, a challenge for change, a stimulus, a lesson, or a shift of priorities.

A doctor directing a clinic insisted that all her staff go through the following exercise. Try it yourself before using it with students fourth grade and up. On a blank sheet of paper, draw a line down the center. On the left, list the thoughts you can remember thinking more than once in the past week. Take time to allow the main ones to emerge. Many are likely to carry an upbeat flavor while others are negative, meshed with an unhappy feeling. Among students they sound like this:

- "I don't want to be here."
- "I hate my little sister."
- "My stepfather doesn't like me and is always ordering me around."
- "I can't wait until X happens."
- "My mother is dumb."
- "I feel awkward and probably look foolish to other people."
- "The teacher doesn't know what's going on."
- "Those kids are mean."
- "I have too much to do and can't handle it."
- "I'm bored out of my mind."
- "I worry about my friends."
- "I worry about my mother."

After jotting your habitual thoughts on the left, weigh the tone of each. Some are already proactive, positive, or express a good feeling—people you love, things you like, worthy aspirations, or affirmations of your ability. Transfer these to the column on the right.

Convert each remaining one into a go-to thought you can substitute in that situation. For every, "I'm helpless" try a constructive thought like "I can at least do this." "So-and-so bugs me" becomes "I can release. . . ." "I'm angry at . . ." may be altered to "I can see that they have a good intention." "I'm worried about . . ." might change to "I think better when I'm calm." "I'm afraid that . . ." changes to "I can handle it when it comes up."

The go-to thought, again, *applies to exactly the same situation* but enhances courage, takes charge, or affirms a learning. Much standard advice amounts to turning our mind *away from* a setting—asking us to count to ten or move our thoughts to a restful place. While this may ameliorate the moment, it can also leave the triggering perception intact so that we are startled later to be harpooned by the same thought.

We solve this by substituting an alternate *first* thought in the situation. The setting may not change, but if we change, we respond differently. Students discussing how to handle a bully on the playground role-played surrounding him and tickling him while reminding him of good things about himself. The strategy constituted a 180-degree shift in their attitude, but they never had to use it because the boy changed on his own just by working with ideas suggested to him.

Students typically know whether they can employ a retooled thought when the time comes, whether they have the power to choose the substitute in place of the original. For the negatives listed above, their replacement might go like this, which you would jot in the right column opposite the original:

- "Since I have to be here, I might as well use the time."
- "My little sister has lots of energy I can help channel."
- "My stepfather wants to keep me out of trouble."
- "Time passes faster if I focus on what I'm doing."
- "Maybe I can learn something from doing this."
- "I need to try things even if I'm uncomfortable at first."
- "The opinions of people who don't care about me aren't important to me."
- "I can give the teacher a heads-up on what's going on behind his back."

The final step of the activity is to combine all the ideas listed in the right column into a smooth summary paragraph. Every day for a couple weeks give them a few moments to read it and think how to apply it. Ask them to read it on their own whenever an old negative idea returns. It helps them regain the stance from which they handle challenges better and also guides your own intervention: "How did your thinking veer off track?" or "What new piece should we add to your summary?"

If they do not consciously correct their mediocre, unproductive thinking, they inescapably recycle it. Cleaning up even one key thought, they begin to manage their life with increased awareness. Small changes making them more successful encourage them to tackle harder problems. Six steps, again, describe the method:

1. Draw a line down a sheet of paper.
2. List their dozen most repeated thoughts on the left.
3. Transfer positives to the right column.
4. Change the remaining negatives to positives and record them on right.
5. Synthesize all positives into a paragraph.
6. Read it daily or whenever an element of it is challenged.

SUMMARY

1. A Consult invites all students to respond briefly to a single question.
2. In Opening a Day, we invite students to notice and share the feeling they bring.
3. Students need competence in understanding and managing a range of feelings.
4. Slowing down a feeling can gradually bring it under control.
5. Suggest a worthy idea to a student and help him track his application of it.
6. Invite students daily to acknowledge others who were friendly to them.
7. A list of positive behaviors can be drawn on in several ways.
8. K–1 students can learn to answer questions by the Two Lines method.
9. Students are unsafe mainly because teachers judge students and students judge each other.
10. Arrange for students to practice listening to and recalling others' words.
11. Teach older students to give total attention to each other without diverting into their own thoughts.
12. Students can learn impulse control with choices at different stages of an experience.
13. Correct thinking by identifying ineffective thoughts and replacing them with better ones.

NOTES

1. Saville Sax and Sandra Hollander, *Reality Games* (New York, Warner Books, 1972). The authors explained this useful idea but gave it an unfortunate name; I retitle here as "Consult."

2. The Gottman Relationship Institute at www.gottman.com offers information on services, research, and products.

3. James M. Kauffman et al., "Friendly Persuasion," *Human Behavior,* September 1977.

4. David Ginsburg, "Quest for the Best Questioning Strategy: Cold Calling vs. Choral Response," *Education Week Teacher* (Online), June 19, 2011. Ginsburg suggests several useful aspects to consider in applying choral response to classroom objectives.

5. If students should find out from a partner an experience of abuse, neglect, or other serious issue, they should already know school protocols for bringing this to the attention of a teacher or staff member. It abandons students in their most dire need if we defer implementing an experience of deep listening on the basis that someone *might* bring such an issue to light.

6. Training in this technique is available from The National Institute for Relationship Enhancement (www.nire.org) which offers many excellent age-specific and general methods and a valuable set of communication skills.

7. Connecting words and ideas to their critical location in the mind is basic to Neuro-Linguistic Programming. The section Correcting Thoughts attempts to pinpoint key ideas and make this substitution at a time when reflection and choice are most easily engaged.

FIVE

Practice with the Imagination

Drawing most benefit from imagination

Imagination is a bigger player in most students' inner world than educators typically attend to.[1] You might hear a child talk to an imaginary friend at play. She commands a world where she can express her needs symbolically. Arranging a group of dolls, children often project their own experience onto them and try out varied dynamics without fear of displeasing adults.

When tense, any of us might use imagination to decompress. We daydream and let our imagery range widely for what restores balance. Nightly we resolve our conflicts by dreaming, and if allowed to, our imagination tries to do the same for us while we are awake. We would like to enable children to draw on it to shape their inner world, guide their behavior, and solve problems instead of projecting their fears onto a dark closet or under their bed.

LIMITS OF MEMORY

To the extent that schools draw on it at all, imagination is usually enlisted for memory techniques rather than self-help. But once into memory, we are confined to the experience we recall and find it harder to allow the novel perspectives that might enhance well-being. If you propose a park and they imagine one they remember, they are limited to what occurred there and are less likely to symbolize freshly something urgent for them.

Their memory may never have registered a sharp sense of falling, for instance, but if imagination supplies one as they play at an imaginary park, it may be trying to work out an issue that feels unsafe to them. If a big, threatening dog approaches in their mind's eye, they may want to resolve a fear—of dogs or something else.

A teacher inquiring about an imagined dog might ask, "So what did you and the dog do?" Maybe the student saw that the owner had the dog on a leash, or ran to his mother, or made friends with the dog, or used a magic wand to turn the big dog into a little one. The experience becomes useful as he can picture his concerns in a way that enables his mind to deliberate on how to handle them symbolically.

INNATE VALUING PROCESS

Such benefits from the imagination appear to be propelled by a little-discussed facet of human nature, its orientation to help itself by all means possible. If you should happen to stumble, why do you try to catch yourself instead of trusting that falling is okay?

Somehow the brain automatically presumes that noninjury is better than injury. In the stumble response, a fundamental human trait is at work, the familiar innate valuing process, our orientation to enhance ourselves. We look for gain as we understand it, asking, "What makes me happier, better, safer, healthier, more successful?"

If this intent were not constantly in play, we could reasonably expect to see many random suicides because people would not assume to start with the idea that life was better than death. Even people who commit suicide think, "I'm better off dead." Their innate valuing process is at work in their last moment, trying to help them improve themselves!

Practice with two conditions increases the help from imagination. One is maintaining continuity inside it, and the other is engaging purposefully with what occurs, like a waking dream we somewhat guide. Picture yourself *inside* a walk down a forest path that you imagine in detail so that the trail and trees hold their place as you pass among them. If you then cease forming details intentionally, what happens?

Your mind does not suddenly go blank. With even a little intent to sustain it, imagination moves onward. It gropes steadily both to notice and create what comes next, and in so doing invents an experience. It might present a moment of beauty, come upon a family reunion, stumble across a wild animal that flees or another that threatens. It might picture the main concern it wants you to address that you find hard to put into words, like a feeling of uneasiness, a fear, a sense of limitation, or a worry. We look next at ways to engage this capacity.

THE CONTROL ROOM

A good start for students' imagination is to take them into the Control Room. They close their eyes and imagine sitting inside their head in a swivel chair. From there they first imagine looking to the front and estimate how far it is out to their eyes.

Then they turn the chair to look out their left ear, estimate the distance, and do the same to the back of their head and right ear. They tilt the chair back to look up, check the distance to the top of their head, and then look down inside their body. You can then conduct a quick Consult about one or more of the distances, like "How far was it out to your left ear?" Only imagination can create the distance.

You can use this exercise to focus them quickly. Begin it with a signal you reserve only for this purpose such as clapping your hands, or say the same words each time, like "Control Room everyone!" Time to the second how quickly they can drop what they're doing, enter there, and go silent. At their own pace, ask them to look in all six directions and then either open their eyes and look at you, or picture an image you designate like, "Science book, please!" As they practice doing this, they realize that their mind is a tool they can direct at will.

FINISH A STORY

Read the opening of a story and then ask, "What happens next? Close your eyes and carry on the story." Or invite them to brainstorm characters about whom they could write a story, and pick one. They see their character in some situation and then turn loose the continuing inner experience until either it ends spontaneously or you ask them to close it.

DEBRIEF

A debrief can affirm the meaning in any activity but is especially important for imagination work because their effort is invisible. Typically something happens, and they open their eyes ready to relate it in any of five ways. Writing and picture drawing are two but require more time and return students to themselves.

Two other styles use verbal response to draw on peer interest. In one, with a small class and students accustomed to listening, you can call on each in turn or respond to hands raised. This helps you know each student better and identify follow-up needed. Each experience they have or comment they make, you imply, was perfect.

An older or larger class may be impatient listening to everyone and need a teacher's affirmation less. You might satisfy their needs by dividing them into pairs or threes to decompress their immediate desire to talk, followed by a few minutes of whole-class discussion.

Finally, if time is limited, you might aim just to elicit a sense of group accomplishment. Pick an element everyone can respond to with a word or phrase, and ask for a show of hands or use a Consult. If, for example, you started them on a sandy beach and they each had their own experience with it, you can ask, "Was the sky blue or cloudy?" "Was the water calm or wavy?" "How many gained a good feeling?" "How many experienced a fearful feeling?"

MANAGE THE IMAGINATION

Few people realize the power they have over the details of their images. Ask students to form a picture of their story character or any image they prefer and lead them through changes to its submodalities.[2] A small percentage find it hard to form a picture and apply these changes but not because of "not trying hard enough." The ability comes naturally or does not.

With eyes closed they make the following changes to their image one at a time. Ask them to nod when they complete it to signal that they are ready for the next alteration. First, they draw a picture frame around their character. When they can do that, bring the picture big and close, and then move it small and far away. Change it from black and white to color or vice versa. Make it bright and flashy, dim it out slowly, restore it to big and bold, give it all one color. Make it move like an action picture, turn it upside down, bounce it. Give it a sound track with slow music, and then make the sound bright and fast. Add voices. Walk into the picture themselves, join the action, shake hands with the character, tell the character they have just created them, and follow out how they respond.

When they open their eyes, discuss what they noticed. Help them realize that in changing an image, *they alter how they represent their life conditions.* Redesigning any image that bothers them, they increase their control over their inner world. A way to handle an annoying picture, for example, is to shrink it into a dot and hurl it off into space until it disappears.[3]

For someone who bothers them, they might color their image pink, turn it upside down, and bounce it until they can laugh about it. When they want to learn a skill, they can apply the submodalities that depict it exactly as it will be when mastered. It may help to see it from two angles—one as a camera looking through their eyes and another as an objective view from the side or above. To concentrate better, they might imagine themselves at their desk with a light beam on them and a sound-proof bubble shield around them that eliminates distractions.

LEAD-IN STEPS

Because few know how to get their imagination moving, Lead-In Steps can help. Tired students go to sleep with this exercise, so do it when everyone is alert. Ask them to sit comfortably at their desk, put their head on their arms, relax, close their eyes, and picture a scene *they have not visited before.* Explain that they are free to follow out the scene as it spontaneously unfolds. They may be drawn to a certain direction, or an object may come to their awareness, or they may feel a nudge toward a specific activity. They just stay aware of the scene until it evolves.

Their imagination may pose challenges. Tell them, "If you encounter a problem, use your imagination to figure out a way to solve it that works in the setting you're in. If you need something, invent it or find it. Be courageous and resourceful." For starting off on different occasions, you might say:

- "You are standing on brightly colored rocks that sparkle in the sun. Notice if you would like to pick up any and look at them."
- "You are hiding in tall grass, and hear children's voices. If you would like to crawl through the grass and join them, go ahead."
- "Look at your hands, the clothes you have on, what is right around you."
- "Look down and feel your feet in sand, and warm water coming over them."
- "Start walking on a new pathway, and notice what draws your attention. Decide if you would like to sit down or keep going."
- "You are in a field and notice a big tree nearby. If you would like to climb it, go ahead."
- "Turn in a circle, and choose which direction you want to walk."
- "The color blue floats in front of you, something big and blue. See what it turns into."

There is no limit to possible beginnings if you can avoid locking them into a memory. They might walk along a new beach, climb an unknown mountain, sit near a remote waterfall, lean against a tree, cross a stream, or continue a dream they had. Pose an image *of something they have never seen* for them to enter, and then have them proceed with it on their own. Focus them on any part of the scene and draw their attention to details that gradually provide color and form. With the character they selected above, you might say:

Close your eyes now, and look at your person. Take your time. Start with their hands, and work out from there. Notice their hair . . . their shoes (or feet) . . . their clothes . . . the look on their face. Now imagine stepping up to them. Say, 'Let's do something together.' Imagine you and them going and doing it.

Sometimes students have a rich and varied experience within a couple minutes. When several appear to have ended, say to everyone, "Please complete the experience with your inner friend soon, and when you're ready, open your eyes." It may take them a minute to wind down. If you have time for a debrief, they narrate in turn what happened to them, everyone listens, and you thank each.

To deepen their experience as you introduce a picture, at some point *mention a detail for each of the three senses*—a sound to hear, something to look for or observe; wind, sun, water, or an object or surface to touch or feel. As you introduce an element, pause and ask them to nod if they grasp it to affirm that they are on track.

Try not to insert details they may already have defined. Instead offer a category certain to be present and let them choose the detail. If you picture them walking, you might say, "Notice what you are standing on, what is underfoot." If they were already moving along a country road, it would jar them to have you specify warm sand.

Practice will help you grasp how fast to go. After a couple minutes of suggesting points for them to notice, let them proceed on their own. While at the start you direct their attention to specific sensations to get them going, this changes once the imagery sustains itself. Turn them loose to focus on whatever comes up, and suggest they cover their ears so they are not interrupted by comments you make to the others.

THE CAVERN BEGINNING

A beginning that never ends the same and so can be used repeatedly is entering a cavern. They close their eyes, and you begin: "Can you imagine a cavern you have never seen before? (Wait until they nod.) Can you stand in front of its entrance? Notice if the rock is dark or light. Go in two steps, and touch the side of it. Is it cold or warm? Wet or dry? Rough or smooth?"

Since they never saw the cavern before, their imagination must define each quality, planting them inside the picture. Then "Feel inside for a handrail. Is it metal or wood?" Slowly count them down six steps and have them look back through the entrance: "Turn and look back. Can you see the light coming through the entrance?" Continue rhythmically down another fourteen steps to a landing. Then suggest that on their own they follow the tunnel into whatever unfolds.

Circulate among them to help them solve problems. With their eyes remaining closed, they can raise their hand. Ask them quietly to tell you the problem they encounter, and explore ways they might solve it by using their imagination. If they face a locked door, they might look for a key. If their tunnel is dark, they could turn on a light. If they encounter a deep pit, help them parachute into it or throw a ladder across it. They sense what they want to do, and you help invent the means: "Would it work to find a light switch and flick it on?"

INTERNAL AWARENESS

Once generating a positive emotional atmosphere in class, you would like to be able to call it up later to help them bring themselves under control, focus on learning, or balance distracting emotions. One way is focusing them on details of their internal experience. Suggest, "Make a space in your right leg," and in turn, do the same at a moderate pace with each limb and their body trunk. This typically creates a light, relaxed feeling entirely produced by their imagination.

You can also direct their attention to microperceptions of their physical state: "Please close your eyes. Now notice how the chair feels under you. Just allow yourself to feel heavier (lighter) in it." Typically as you direct their attention to such feelings, they will notice what you suggest. The important feature of the experience is that they practice *observing* themselves and then *managing* the direction of their attention. If they can observe themselves getting lighter, they could also watch as their attention narrows into a laser beam to apply to the next lesson or as they imagine their emotions like a gyroscope in perfect balance.

Practice in directing awareness is a valuable step toward managing their emotional life. Have a daily minute in which they survey themselves and notice any prominent feeling. Often unhappiness shows in tension in the stomach or throat, or pressure on the chest. Ask students, "Does anyone have 'elephant chest' this morning?"

When they inquire what that is, tell them, "It's the feeling of an elephant standing on your chest." If they are not able to release it directly, they can at least give it calm, caring attention. Tell them, "Sit with it like a doctor at the bedside of a sick patient. Allow it to change slowly. Invite your deeper mind to help by telling it, 'I allow myself to feel better.'" Letting them narrate internal sensations or imaginary experiences to another as they occur can help the experience continue.

SUMMARY

1. Imagination can be enlisted for personal problem solving.
2. Help students create a Control Room inside their head.
3. Let imagination finish a story you begin for them.
4. Debriefs can help confirm the gains from imagination activities.
5. Teach them how to change the submodalities of their inner pictures.

6. As students enter an imagined scene and sustain it, a helpful experience can unfold.
7. Walking students into a cavern is a standard beginning that never ends the same.
8. Observing microperceptions of their inner state can aid their self-management.

NOTES

1. Jacob Bronowski, *The Origins of Knowledge and Imagination* (New Haven, CT: Yale University Press, 1978). Bronowski advances a thought-provoking explanation of the role of imagination in the formation of knowledge. We aim at an elusive layer of attention in students as we try to understand, "How are you imagining this?" Students do not *receive* meaning ready-made. To make it their own, they must invent it by an imaginative process.

2. Anthony Robbins, *Unlimited Power* (New York: Fawcett Columbine, 1986). For a detailed explanation of the meaning and use of submodalities, see chapter 6: Mastering Your Mind: How to Run Your Brain, page 83ff.

3. In Neuro-Linguistic Programming this useful idea is known as "the Swish Technique." Robbins explains it in detail in *Unlimited Power*, on page 100.

SIX

Practice Sustaining Attention

Hold students' attention steadily

Many students are immersed in their own isolated world and find it hard to express themselves constructively and feel received. Once believing they are socially unsuccessful, they may refuse to do more than answer a teacher's direct question and lose out entirely on the gains from exchange with their peers. To allay fear and generate participation, our key must lie in directing their effort. What can we ask of them that gets them confidently attending to, thinking about, and building on what others say?

For many classroom issues we need to 1) understand the problem, 2) identify the *behavior* that corrects it, 3) ask for the behavior, and 4) arrange for success and good feelings from it.

1. *Understand the problem.* Our problem here is students who are isolated and unable to connect with peers. Examining why, we note that typical classroom management constantly returns student attention to the teacher. *By our design,* students speak *to the teacher* rather than to each other, so what should we expect?

2. *Identify the behavior that corrects it.* To correct that, we arrange for students to connect with what other students say instead of (or in addition to) responding to the teacher. Instead of everyone looking to the teacher to be called on next, they need to look at each other and join their comment to what was already said.

3. *Ask for the behavior.* Challenge students to produce a class list of "ways to connect with another student's idea." The list might include recall it, summarize it, praise it, compliment it, add to it, modify it, include it in something else, correct it, ask permission to move on from it, challenge it, and argue with it.

4. *Arrange for success and good feelings from it.* The crucial phase is enabling them to do these things successfully with good feelings. You can divide the class into groups of three to five and ask them to talk about anything they wish (or you can select a topic). Drawing on the means they brainstorm, they are to *connect each of their comments to something already said.* You might suggest, "Aim to link up ideas as though you were weaving a tapestry together." As they are able to do this in small groups, they rapidly adapt it to larger numbers. The aim of relating to a prior idea causes everyone's idea to matter to others, leading them more directly to experience inclusion and think more carefully about what they say.

While this approach might be welcomed from the second grade up, younger children may have no ideas they want to express. Some may be passive, others dominant, and the class distracted. Assuming you are willing to work a little harder, what else could you do?

HUMAN DEVELOPMENT PROGRAM

An innovation over forty years ago demonstrated the powerful influence of a style of group leadership seldom found in schools today. Few back then acknowledged that we must address students' feelings and relationships and that doing so could transform learning. the Human Development Program (HDP) then was pioneering aspects of this understanding, beginning with the principle that *feelings are the prime movers of behavior.*[1]

Its manner of recognizing and building on children's feelings and personal experiences had a deep impact on them, leading even first graders with a year in the program to confident self-awareness and interpersonal skills. Its premise went like this: In order to reach children, we need to connect with them through what they truly own, something that represents themselves. Complying with school demands is not enough. Most ideas they encounter in school originate with someone else and for that reason can be hard for them to invest in. As their experience diverges from the school's emphasis, they more readily disconnect from it.

Their feelings, however, are theirs alone. If an experience made them sad, they know the feeling is theirs. If happy, they are the one happy, and likewise if they are anxious, embarrassed, joyful, pressured, or hopeful. Nothing is more personal than their feeling, and they draw a straight line conclusion: *How their feeling is treated is how they are treated.* How you respect my feeling is how you respect me. Our handling of their vulnerable inner world manifests our love for them.

Once connected to them we have a doorway through which to help them develop self-management, effective social behavior, and then knowledge. We bridge into their sometimes amorphous inner world and work respectfully with what we find.

DESIGN FOR SHARING

The design of the HDP drew on how feelings attach to experiences students can narrate. Daily for fifteen to twenty minutes, a teacher would introduce a topic from the many ways people give and receive good feelings, experience life, exercise personal capabilities, and become successful. Shy children with even a one-word answer to whisper to the teacher could participate. Because the form of this sharing offers an enduring lesson, it is presented here in some detail.

The teacher first announces a topic and pauses. When the teacher says, "A time I got a good feeling from an animal . . ." anyone might raise his or her hand. Only one talks at a time. The teacher calls on Jennifer, who might say, "I play with my kitten." She thanks Jennifer and asks the question again. This time Aaron volunteers. She calls on him and he says, "I like to wrestle with my dog." The next turn is with Jeff, who says, "My dog waits for me and always comes to the door when I come back home."

If some do not have pets, maybe they went to a zoo or watched an animal perform, or may decline to participate that day. The basic theme of *the causes of good feelings* recurs constantly. Everyone is free to share, everyone who shares is listened to, and the cue is open rather than restrictive.

What might students conclude from the three answers above? Easy to overlook is that *students learn a conclusion best by drawing it themselves from their own experience.* Any single answer may seem of minor import, but children's minds connect them. Implied are that 1) everyone has good feelings, 2) good feelings are important, 3) good feelings are caused, 4) they come from many different directions, 5) everyone's feeling is valid, and 6) you can cause good feelings in yourself and others. No one needs to pound home these life-changing realizations because students grasp them on their own. Imagine *telling* them to students. Their influence lies instead in students *noticing* them as a quality of their personal activity.

And while topics about pets might show up more often in elementary level material, such ordinary, common themes carry a message for all ages. High school students would likely respond to the same one. Good feelings do not depend on exceptional events or arcane insight. A topic's value lies not in uniqueness or complexity but rather in how familiar experience conveys essential understanding.

Thinking what to do *after* the three responses above, teachers might throw up their hands and declare, "At that point, I'd lose everyone!" foreseeing students chattering about their times with animals and order breaking down. So how do we maintain continued attention?

At one level we can suspend the activity. "Use it or lose it" is a fallback. The teacher might say, "Maybe we're too distracted today to do this. We can try again tomorrow," implying, "We're going to keep at this till we get it right." The teacher lays out the ground rules, the experience continues as long as the rules are followed, the next day the rules are re-presented, all agree to them, and the experience resumes.

But the approach creates its own attention when the teacher paces the sharing *no faster than everyone in the group can remember what everyone else says*. After the third response, the teacher might suggest a review. "Let's see where we have come. Who can remember who shared first?" Some-one says "Jennifer!" and the teacher responds with "Congratulations! You were paying attention," and continues with "And who can remem-ber *how* Jennifer got good feelings from an animal?"

The teacher looks around the group. Who listened carefully enough to recall what Jennifer said? A hand goes up and someone answers, "She plays with her kitten." The teacher smiles and answers, "Thank you Mon-ica! You were *listening*!" She goes on: "Who can remember how Aaron got good feelings with an animal?" A hand goes up, and Joe says, "Aaron wrestles with his dog."

Again the teacher congratulates the effort and thanks Joe. Finally, "And who can remember how Jeff got good feelings?" The answer comes from Michael: "His dog welcomes him home." The teacher thanks Mi-chael.

Jennifer, Aaron, and Jeff were reinforced by *being* remembered and hence had a reason to listen carefully to find out how others accounted for them. Monica, Joe, and Michael were reinforced *for* remembering. The messages minute by minute told everyone, "You're on track; you're all succeeding!" Others knew that at any moment 1) they might contribute something others would respect and remember, 2) they might be recog-nized for what they shared before, and 3) they might be the one recalling what others say.

KEY TEACHER ROLE

While for students the activity conveys ease and social bonding, the teacher must be focused, attending steadily to students' ongoing atten-tion—Monica said this, Jose said that, Gracie was next, and so on. By inviting students to remember everything, the teacher commits to the same. Once the topic connects with them personally and their answers are valid, the intermittent review reinforces their effort to remember.

A typical class honors only the teacher's words, but when the class must recall only what the teacher says, *neither the teacher nor students need to pay attention to anyone else!* A student comment may create momentary noise but rapidly recede into oblivion.

Changing this pattern is a watershed. When the goal instead is that everyone remembers everyone, teachers must make everyone's offering significant instead of just their own. They make a constant review of their own recall of each participant, so that upon proposing to the circle of students, "Let's see how far we've come. Who can remember . . . ?" they *know* what comes next.

The impact on students makes this urgent. Those most likely to escape notice are the shy who speak briefly and softly. The effect on them when everyone but them is remembered is as though *intending* a lethal discount. The teacher conducts a continuing internal review to make sure she keeps clearly in mind everything said, which is the increment of her effort that ensures children's success.

DEVISING TOPICS

Insight about a topic is a secondary goal. Our primary goal of the activity is to give the most hesitant the confidence to speak, find good feelings in their own experience, and recognize their own strengths of understanding. For this, simple topics work that spring from their own experience and actions. Children take enormous interest in simple, concrete things. Could not any of us, for example, expound at length on "cuts and bruises when I was young"?

To devise a bank of topics, have a brainstorming session with them to name things they would like to talk about. This should quickly give you a list of single words that fit their age. Then turn each word into a topic constructed like this:

- "An experience I had with . . ."
- "A good feeling that came from . . ."
- "How I solved a problem with . . ."
- "How I got better at . . ."

Your aim is just to form the topic to make it easy for them to respond to. One can readily imagine kindergartners telling their own story about "an experience I had with my *toothbrush*."[2] Think how vivid certain presences can appear in their minds, like a favorite toy, their yard, a blanket, a stairway, and so on.

A helpful category is addressing feelings they have experienced (cf., chapter 4 for two lists). For positive ones, phrase the topic as "A time I felt . . ." Students then tell their experience in response to the topic, with the goal, again, just of having everyone accept and acknowledge the incident each one narrates. Their initial need is met by the group appreciating what each shares, rather than by insight into whys and wherefores.

For negative feelings, phrase it as, "A problem I solved about . . ." or "A challenge I faced with. . . ." Whatever the topic, continue to look for how they 1) generate good feelings from common experience, 2) demonstrate capabilities, 3) solve problems, and 4) remember what others say.

See the appendices in *Effective Classroom Turnaround: Practice Makes Permanent* for age-related lists of topics.

GO FOR IT

One adaptation to address children's social-emotional needs was based on discussing a couple dozen feelings likely to turn up in their lives. A teacher used the design for an hour a week with a class of upper elementary students assigned to her because of ongoing behavior problems.

She concluded each session by asking, "Okay, who's ready to *go for it?*" meaning *"Who would like to recount what everyone said from the beginning of the hour?"* All then listened in silence as one student carefully summarized what everyone had contributed. By the end of her series, her students' behavior problems had evaporated. They shifted basic attitudes by expressing their own thoughts and feelings as others listened carefully, responded to them, and remembered them.[3]

A teacher can draw on this critical mind-set to encourage students' attention to all learning. Expect everyone to remember everything said, and celebrate all attempts to demonstrate that.

Have a cup of wooden craft sticks with students' names on them. After you elicit a few responses from students about the subject of the day, draw a name and ask the student if they can recall the comment made a minute before by another student. If they can't, no matter. If they can, give verbal praise: "You were listening," "Right on!" "Way to go!" "On top of it!" "Good going," and so on. As you do this throughout the period, point out that they are building cumulative retention of everything said. Explain how important a life skill this will be.

SUMMARY

1. Children assume that how their feeling is treated is how they are treated.
2. Students learn a conclusion best by drawing it from their own experience.
3. Devise topics from common experiences of good feelings, exercising capabilities, and problem solving.
4. Pace the sharing in a group no faster than everyone can recall what everyone else says.
5. The teacher must remember continually what each student shares.
6. When students must pay attention only to what the teacher says, they need not pay attention to anyone else.
7. Ask students to link their comment to something said earlier.

8. With older students, conclude a period by asking one student to summarize everything said.

NOTES

1. The Human Development Program expanded into an array of resources for social-emotional learning, available now at InnerChoice Publishing, 15079 Oak Chase Court, Wellington, FL 33414, info@innerchoicepublishing.com. A significant contribution to its early effectiveness were the carefully designed daily topics that opened up many distinctions children grapple with in order to understand their experience. Here, for better or worse, we leave it to teacher and students to expand understanding around topics of common experience they select.

2. I dropped it on the floor and it got all dirty; I was playing with it and my mother put it away and forgot where she put it; my dog got it and chewed it all up; I tried to stuff it down the drain and my mom was all upset; I was running around with it in my mouth and my brother tried to take it away from me and hurt my mouth; I put too much toothpaste on it and it fell off and made a big lump in the sink; the toothpaste tasted so good that I'd eat some every night until my dad caught me.

3. Thanks to Ann Whitelaw for developing and demonstrating the impact of this valuable technique.

SEVEN

Draw on Social Roots

Students cue each other's learning

Few circumstances affect learning more powerfully than students' desire for attention from each other and the teacher. Often they do not know how to express their enormous energy constructively but depend on our guidance to show them how. If we can harness their grasping for attention and acceptance, we have a potential powerhouse at our disposal.

When and why they talk is an issue. Many teachers fail to recognize that students must talk about ideas to assimilate them and instead occupy themselves with preparing their class for standardized testing. Their main effort is to get testable answers into students' heads while deferring assimilation as an extra that can wait.

A quantity of quiet work is essential, of course. With it, students gather and organize what they will absorb later. But if later outcomes are not pursued, seat work may be reduced just to processing disconnected facts and filling in blanks, leaving the field of competent knowledge poor.

ROLE OF TALK

Talking about it is in fact the instinctive way children prefer to absorb fresh knowledge. If they can, they exchange ideas about everything that interests them. Shared interest is the intuitive validator of meaning. If we say something and our friends respond, we conclude that it had worth. If they ignore it, toss their heads, or roll their eyes, we conclude that it did not—a blow to our claim on it. As peers receive ideas we express, we reaffirm our place among them.

Besides building skill, the kind of practice suggested here implies relationship. It is social. Even a question and answer structure requires two people—one asking and one answering—embodying a social value. We assign students to pair up, ask each other the questions, and attest to each other's ability, leveraging their tendency to regard relationships as significant even if this individual was not a friend before.

Since they want to be viewed as competent by their peers, if the task before them is expressing learning, they want to be good at it. In presenting themselves to others, their identity, in a sense, is on the line. Learning, not important for any other reason, becomes so because through it they demonstrate that they deserve others' admiration. For complex material, utilize partner practice chunk by chunk. To save it permanently, set at least a regular weekly time for bringing all past learning up to current competence. They practice what they are weak on to draw it back from oblivion.

During this activity of reclaiming knowledge, when the other receives and understands what they say, a reciprocal loop of affirming energy returns to them, providing immediate satisfaction and bonding them. Doing this with one peer after another, they develop a group norm that "we can talk about math together."

As the teacher says, "Help each other get all the pieces in the right order," comments back and forth have both instructional and social meaning. What one remembers that another does not or what they understand differently spurs an effort to clarify, affirming the assumption that the two can communicate and might even do so during lunch. A correlation holds. *The more students talk in a manner valued by peers, the more they own what they say.*

STANFORD STUDY

While much research and experience show the importance of student talk in general, an aspect pivotal for education received support from a study sponsored by Stanford University.[1]

Encounter groups had become popular at the time, but some participants appeared to benefit while others did not, and the reasons were not evident. To sort out why, the university arranged a comparison of different leadership styles and observed the internal conduct of the groups to discover which influences helped participants both to change positively and maintain their changes over time.

Two findings especially invite our attention. One was that accepting a moderate level of emotional expression aided growth. Cold-blooded classrooms are less likely to enhance learning. Another was that *those who changed most and sustained their changes participated actively, and others regarded their contributions as influential.*

For us, this is like finding a gold nugget in a neighborhood brook. *We can arrange the presence of moderate feelings, for students to express their ideas, and for others to treat them as valuable.* A social context can change a student from shrugging off learning to claiming it personally. Two particular processes help this along.

AUTOBIOGRAPHICAL CODING

This describes claiming an idea as our own. We hold it inside the relatively small inner circle of thoughts important to us *because* we regard them as personal, independent of their objective significance. One student may do this with math, another with dinosaurs, and another with nothing related to school — think video games instead. Students individuate by what they label as "mine."

Encounter groups mattered because their content was personal, about the self. Our question here is how to create such a claim on academic learning, which students first perceive as impersonal and distant from their lives.

We assist that process of claim as we draw on social roots that generate significance from scratch. Helping us out are the "back and forth" of reciprocity and the appeal to peer standards in their desire for competence.[2] If Jeff reads a book about astronomy and narrates it to Jan for five minutes, Jan can verify this to the teacher, who posts the time on a chart by Jeff's name — a cycle of reciprocity and acknowledgment of competence. A significance-creating process gathers up Jeff's effort and gives it an aura of attractiveness, making it easier for Jeff to say, "I love reading about astronomy."

We would prefer of course for Jeff to read without the stimulus, and he might. But there are also many Brians who would not take the extra step on their own but do for a social reason. We arrange follow-up steps that acknowledge the importance of the effort, credit them to the individual, and engage his social relationships.

ACTION SET

This means being poised to act on what they learn. A motive for students to pay attention moment to moment can be a teacher's habit of pausing abruptly and asking a question about what he or she just said. With this, the teacher sustains an Action Set among the students that in turn helps focus them on the presentation.

Similarly if they are about to be tested on it, or must use it in a project, or must share it with someone, they feel the spotlight on them and have a reason for gripping the idea. Anything they foresee acting on, they instinctively want to be competent at doing. *The premier action easily arranged in the classroom hour by hour is explaining the current idea either to a partner at once or later to the entire class.*

These social links comprise a series of clues about children's likelihood of buying into the learning you present: 1) Do they feel emotionally "up" about the learning activity? 2) Are they able to share their own ideas? 3) Do others respond with respect and interest? 4) Do the features of the activity encourage them to claim the learning? 5) Are they about to act on the knowledge presented?

BETTER OUTCOMES FROM READING

A social context stimulates reading.[3] The Study and Share model works well with adults and older students (cf., *Teaching Students to Work Harder and Enjoy It: Practice Makes Permanent*, chapter 15, for more on this technique). With one or two hours available, have everyone choose a book that appeals to each.[4] Interest up front helps ensure their engagement, but the method itself can generate it. For middle and high school students, you can assign books in a subject area. They think differently even about a textbook if they can explore it freely and comment on any part of it.

The activity is comprised of 1) reading silently for ten to twenty minutes, 2) sharing with a partner what they read, and 3) doing the prior steps for several rounds with different partners. The format generates energy for learning and enhances social relationships. Everyone has the maximum talking time if they remain in pairs rather than cluster in groups.

With children five to about eight, the best influence appears to occur by reading aloud to a parent. Beginning readers do not yet read smoothly. Problems of pronunciation and meaning reduce their ability to enjoy the story. They lose the thread, and the reading ceases to satisfy.

A parent listening dignifies the child's effort by receiving it, and the child bonds with them while absorbing ideas and practicing skills. It may be worth a research project to find out if the time taken for homework assignments is better spent just in students of all ages reading to an adult—for all the implications of help, relationship, and idea development that might ensue.

SOCIAL HANDLES

Students' social nature offers many handles for creating good feelings with learning once they get along with peers. We invite them to express their appreciation for how others give them good feelings (cf., Appreciation Time in chapter 4). They notice a good feeling in themselves and its source in another and learn how to support each other, reinforcing behaviors aligned with learning. The method steadily nudges them to be alert to each other as they name who was friendly to them.

The teacher has a social impact. With brief words, looks, and nods, teachers as social participants affirm students' actions that contribute to good feelings, order, and cooperation. A long-term influence is simply that a teacher emits warmth and liking for children.

The behavioral plans students learn for getting along with peers have direct impact as they increasingly understand how to make their actions socially successful and how to reinforce others' positive behavior. Their academic effort likewise becomes social as in pairs they listen to each other explain their learning, making the content of the curriculum a social bridge.

As they rise to their feet, answer questions about social skills, and also demonstrate their academic knowledge, others applaud their performance. They "stand and deliver," receive social affirmation for doing so, and claim knowledge as a personal possession. And once they discover acceptance and respect by expressing genuine knowledge, the sky is the limit. Personal relationships then empower rather than distract from learning. Without this confidence, formal discussions remain on the surface and eventually dissolve into distractive behavior.

Unless students realize that it is safe for them to think, that their thinking connects them with each other, and that it *satisfies* them, the more assertive interrupt and do the talking for everyone. The quieter comply with teacher requests and try to avoid embarrassment.

We draw similarly on their social needs to energize instruction. After they initially learn an idea from you, however you achieve that, four further steps involve their social relationships.

1. *Practice.* With pre-K you can practice in unison, asking the question and hearing everyone's answer. With kindergarten and first grade, we raise the energy by teaching them the Two Lines method above, where one line asks the question and the other answers it. Their learning is socially relevant as they show themselves competent to a peer.

Older students able to follow instructions better can separate into partner pairs and practice asking and answering complex questions. Once they understand the practice format, you can insert any learning into it. *Success lies not just in expressing their learning but also in expressing it after they have learned it well.*

2. *Perform.* Done at the day's end, this reinforcer allows them to leave school feeling successful. Write each question they learn on a separate card or slip of paper and put them in a bag. Place children's names in a different bag or on wooden craft sticks upright in a cup. Daily for a few minutes draw a question and then a name. The student rises to his feet and performs an answer already practiced one to one. When they are

confident that they know the answers, they welcome the chance to demonstrate them.

3. *Applaud.* Nothing quite matches peer applause to let them know they have done something right. It takes but a few seconds, conveys a generalized sense of group approval, and especially benefits the shy.

4. *Score.* Games stimulate students by scoring every advance of their skill. Comparably with individual pieces of learning, you can make up a chart having student names down the left and five columns across for days of the week plus one more for a running total. Under each day, count up the score for each one's new knowledge added that day, a point for each answer or subpoint of a multipoint answer. Maintain a cumulative figure in the last square at the end. Credit them with a tally for every answer or part of one that took independent effort to learn.

As they repeat these steps, it dawns on students that others appreciate their personal competence, and they feel justly proud of their results. The energetic have a focus for their effort, and others a clear path to step up their game.

THE POWER OF PEER CONNECTIONS

Nothing is more certain to students than their own intent to do better when they know peers are watching. The effect is redoubled when they expect that after their attempt they will hear from peers "how they did." We have a motivational powerhouse available and need only wire it to something we want students to learn. Since the setup brings intense focus on specific increments of skill, we can reserve it for important material if time is limited.

The skills below are important for positive communications and are behaviorally *observable.* The third on the list is internal but can be intuited by others.

1. Notice others' desire to speak.
2. Look at the speaker.
3. Feel respect.
4. Wait until they're done.
5. Leave a brief silence.
6. Share your idea.
7. Speak in short messages.
8. Connect to others' ideas.
9. Include everyone.
10. Ask questions.
11. Remember others' ideas.
12. Thank people.
13. Give a compliment.

14. Sum up their ideas.
15. Ask about their feelings.
16. Check your guesses about their thoughts.

Third graders and up can understand the basic meaning of these points, but each one stands at the head of a long continuum of skill development.

To help students practice them, make up a chart on a sheet of paper (landscape works if you use a small font). List the skills down the left edge, and at the top make a space for their name. Fill the space to the right of the skills with quarter-inch columns. Distribute a sheet to each student, and explain how to jot a rating of the skill (on a 1–10 scale) in the appropriate box. Place a date at the top of the first available column, and instruct them to write their name on the sheet. Several activities can help them master it.

1. Read one skill at a time, explain how its use affects communication, and give examples of it. Invite students' experience of having the skill used or not used toward them. As you discuss each skill, invite them to rate their habitual use of it.
2. Divide students into groups of three to five. Read through the list with everyone. Clarify any points they don't understand, and ask each group to agree on a rating for everyone in their group—who is generally good at what. When they are uncertain, suggest that they all accept the same score between 1 and 10.
3. To equalize chances for giving and receiving peer feedback, ask them to count off from 1 to 4 in their group. After the groups talk for five to ten minutes, they then take turns rating everyone in their group (including themselves) by their use of a single skill for that time. For the first skill, student number 1 might assign an 8, two 9s, and a 10 to those in his or her group (one of them a self-rating). Student 2 might give everyone a 10 for the second skill, and so on down the list.
4. Divide them into groups of three. Let them talk for three to five minutes, pause them, and ask them to make a tally mark beside any skill they themselves specifically used in that time. As you do this regularly, point out how the quality of their conversation changes as they use more of the skills toward each other.
5. Verbal feedback has a different impact than a written score. After a brief discussion in small groups, ask them to tell each other specifically which skill they noticed another use. The other then makes a tally by the appropriate skill.
6. With everyone's name at the top of his or her own sheet, the students hand their sheet to their right. After a three to five minute discussion, participants make a tally on the sheet in front of them (bearing another's name) beside any skill they observed that person use.

7. At the end of the school day, ask them to pick one or two skills from the sheet to monitor overnight. The next day, ask them to share with the class skills they observed being used (or not used when they were needed) and what the effect was. You might alternatively ask them to write you a brief note about their observations.

8. Provide them time to memorize the list. Have a class celebration when everyone can tell it back without help.

A PROBLEM-SOLVING METHOD

An axiom informing our approach is first to understand the child. Doing that, we know where to focus our personal authority and control of consequences. Beginning instead with enforcing an instructional design can short-circuit our grasp of the internal dynamics driving their behavior. We have little to lose by taking full account of students' perceived inner world, since doing so may support rule-following better than does narrow reliance on rules. As we are considerate toward their inner state, they reciprocate and attend better to the issue. They first want to know that we value how they perceive, think, and feel, and then cooperate readily with our channel for their energy.

A reasonable rationale for going first to our rule is that, boiled down, it synthesizes multiple agreements about how to fill a need with numbers of students at the same time and can make activity more efficient. As things go wrong, however, such a tack may be *less* efficient. Ordering, coercing, or cajoling students to observe the rule, we may find them continuing to distract, rebel, and sabotage classroom effort.

We might frame such problems as the two fields diverging. Rules say one thing, and their internal experience says another. We require them to adjust to the rule because we regard it as simple and necessary, yet simplicity vanishes as we scan their inner field where they process thousands of thoughts and feelings daily and where their perceived distance from classmates and teacher weighs heavily. For better or worse, they have a stance toward everyone around them and make guesses about their own safety and connection with each one respectively. They are driven to process a flood of details constantly by the ongoing necessity of choosing how to act but often perceive through too narrow a lens, misinterpret a circumstance, or exaggerate a feeling.

Since their constant internal activity has such power to impel their behavior, we need not wait until it is acted out to enable them to handle it constructively. We prefer to head off negative tendencies before they manifest in hurtful actions. While schools may employ many means to help students do this, some teachers invent their own.

Christoff von Gemmingen, a fourteen-year teacher, developed a conflict resolution approach based on a few simple steps. The teacher qualities it draws on are familiar, mainly a sensitive, gentle appreciation of children's inner state (a values component) and an ability to elicit and sort through their problems quickly (a skill component).

His combined class of twenty-seven second and third graders face him in three compact rows. In a cup on his desk are Popsicle sticks with a number on each, which he works through every day. He draws out one at a time, reads the number on it, and the student corresponding to that number stands.

"So Gary," Christoff says, "how was your day today?"

Gary answers first with one word such as "good," "poor," "awesome," or "brilliant." Students are free to choose any label they wish. If they pick an unusual word, Christoff often knows the reason, makes a comment or gives feedback, and continues to his second question.

"Do you have any compliments, complaints, or apologies?" This question is the linchpin of the approach. Gary's answer begins a public but personal, intensive, brief, and if necessary problem-solving conversation between Christoff and Gary, drawing in other class members as needed. The class is expected to recognize and express appreciation for all positive actions, help clarify misunderstandings, and assist in problem solving.

If Gary says he has a compliment, he addresses it to one or several students. Saying, "Thanks to everyone who played with me at recess," he hears calls of "You're welcome, Gary." If the compliment describes someone notably going out of their way to do a kindness, the class applauds.

For the few who voice a complaint about another's action, the aim is to heal and resolve any lingering hurt or distance generated. With the problem described, everyone turns to the other student, who might apologize outright, tell their side, or realize that their action produced an unintended outcome. Occasionally Christoff engages in a rapid-fire series of questions and answers back and forth with a student to uncover a constructive stance they can take or identify an action they agree to carry out.

Children's minds are often capable of rapid and efficient problem solving *if we align with their thinking and perceptions*. Christoff nails this alignment, concluding many issues in less than a minute, though a teacher might resort to a back-up by saying, "Could you and I talk about this later?" Christoff may jot brief notes on the board as a reminder for follow-up. Rarely, if a single student's problem takes up ten minutes, Christoff compacts the exchange with the remaining students.

With a complaint eliciting a denial from another student ("I didn't do that!"), he is careful not to take sides but rather extracts possibilities ("Is it even *possible* that you stepped on his foot as you hurried by?") and invites an apology based on it ("Well, if I did, I'm sorry."). Students involved in gossip often do not realize the effect of their actions. They benefit from nudges to see another's point of view ("How do you think he would feel?"). Complaints might include these:

- Someone didn't want to play with me.
- Someone almost tripped me.
- Someone said what sounded like a putdown.
- Others didn't share.
- Others were talking about me.
- Others didn't give me my turn.
- How someone expressed his or her anger.
- What disappointed them.

When children have no compliments, complaints, or apologies, Christoff makes a point of noting something personal about them—work turned in, praise for their effort, their parents' pleasure in how well they are doing, or changes made since last year. No one escapes personal notice of some kind.

The method leaves students' internal self-management to be dealt with by other activities or by individual counseling and sticks just with their current interpersonal actions. Although they can pick whatever word they want to describe their day, the material elicited further is about their interactions with class members.

This boundary contributes to the rapid disposal of issues and also helps the teacher avoid getting sucked into the arcane features of a single child's perceptions. Because their interactions are the biggest offender distracting from learning, resolving them makes instruction easier and economizes on time. The internal dynamics of the class are both the arena where issues surface and content that can usually be resolved.

Discussing issues in front of others cuts through students' tendencies to evade, distort, or rationalize. The reaction of everyone around them listening to every word they say is an intuitive baseline of social reality. Witnesses quickly straighten out any one-sided story. All relevant parties are present for each issue, so that they can be opened, addressed, and disposed of directly. The process repeated day by day generates a powerful ethic with lifetime application: *Whatever your problem with others, face it and resolve it.*

Three conditions appear essential for children's cooperation. The first is *safety* conveyed by an atmosphere of care and considerateness. Students know they feel better afterward than before. No one is put down or excluded. None is disrespected. Even those who acted improperly are relieved that the issue is behind them. Safety arises in turn from *competence,* the teacher's ability to see through their games and call them to account for any unkindness, yet as a mentor in problem solving rather than a top sergeant giving orders.

Students cannot open their vulnerability if they foresee their attempt leaving them worse off—if others roll their eyes or whisper a putdown—so the two prior conditions are important for encouraging a third. In the presence of safety and competence, children still need *courage* to put into words what troubles them or gives them good feelings and actually say the words to others involved.

It can take courage to tell what happened to you, hope that others will treat it respectfully, and believe that it can be solved, but their courage is quickly rewarded. Putting words to their perceptions and speaking them out loud objectifies them, separating them from the self and turning them into a focus for conscious, objective deliberation.

The issues children bring up are not a random draw from all human experience. They arise instead from a more manageable set driven by the need to know where we stand with others, the Fundamental Interpersonal Relations Orientation factors of affection, inclusion, and control.[5] Students live these drives, and minute by minute want to know: How close am I to others? Am I accepted? What influence do I have? With these uncertainties constantly in play to color their experience, children are compelled to try to figure them out. The factors drive their fears, their tentative guesses about how to get along, and what they dare attempt. Because of their pivotal activity, they deserve at least brief daily attention.

Christoff typically spends fifteen minutes a day with the method and has used it in grades one through six. He says that it works with them all but adds, "It's *especially* effective in the sixth grade where they get so wrapped up in gossip." Since the factors involved are common to all ages, the method should apply as well in upper grades and high school where interpersonal strategies can become more convoluted and in greater need of remedy. It drastically reduces distractions from learning and makes transitions between activities smoother and faster. Students give better attention and avoid a host of behavioral issues.

SUMMARY

1. The more people talk in a way peers value, the more they own what they say.
2. Those who change most and sustain their changes participate actively, and others view their contributions as influential.
3. We need to supply the conditions for autobiographical coding, claiming an idea as one's own.
4. Being poised to act on what they learn motivates students' efforts.
5. The premier action easily arranged is explaining the current idea to someone else.

6. Study and Share can interest students in reading and enhance relationships.
7. Try to arrange for young students to read to their parents.
8. Success is not just in expressing their learning but also in doing so after they have learned it well.
9. Basic learning steps have social impact: practice, perform, applaud, and score.
10. Daily ask students if they have any compliments, complaints, or apologies.

NOTES

1. Morton A. Lieberman, Irving Yalom, and Matthew Miles, *Encounter Groups: First Facts* (New York: Basic Books, 1973).

2. Jerome S. Bruner, *The Process of Education,* 25th printing (Cambridge, MA: Harvard University Press, 1960). Twenty-fifth printing in 1999. The power of these two processes named first by Bruner has long been acknowledged. The question is how to activate them in the classroom. Our design here for practicing knowledge is one way. In other sections we comment also on Bruner's two other intrinsic motives for learning, curiosity, and identification with adults or peers.

3. Kelly Gallagher, *Readicide: How schools are killing reading and what you can do about it* (Portland, ME: Stenhouse Publishers, 2011). Gallagher's treatment of how standard instruction kills students' desire to read aligns with our emphasis here. The book is a helpful tool for a school devising the reading program they want.

4. This method presumes that your students have already developed a certain freedom of expression. For help in this skill area, see Perfect Conversation method in *Teaching Students to Work Harder and Enjoy It: Practice Makes Permanent* or the Communication Skills Check Sheet in *Effective Classroom Turnaround: Practice Makes Permanent.* A child's lack of interest in *anything* speaks more to unmet emotional needs than genuinely reflecting their interests. They all await someone else who really understands them. You might use the time when others are reading to engage them in conversation. Elicit more about their mental field and consider their activities that might suggest a book. Aim first to make it easy for them to narrate anything they read. If they have seen a movie or watched a sport, find a book matching it.

5. William C. Schutz, *FIRO : A Three Dimensional Theory of Interpersonal Behavior* (New York: Holt, Rinehart, & Winston, 1958.)

EIGHT

Alter Thinking to Gain Order

Change behavior by changing thinking

A kindergartner suspended for being physical with classmates and not cooperating may still greet the teacher with a hug and a smile to begin the day. He still expects life to be good but misunderstands how to pursue it.

The suspension and other consequences may get his attention, but once we have it, is it enough that he ceases to hit? His mistaken ideas may go underground and re-emerge later in forms not punished as directly. He is more likely to prosper as his thinking straightens out.

PRESERVING OUR VALUES

Our manner of pressing him to change may actually close his mind to us and make misbehavior more likely. A desperate teacher said, "The moment I let up, the class just disintegrates." He felt he could not do without a loud voice, severe tones, and threats, yet the behavior of his class did not change.

Such methods can undermine important values. Students often feel at the mercy of forces they cannot control, not least their own unhappy feelings and life circumstances. We can reinforce these limitations by how we accuse them of wrongdoing; re-immerse them in feelings of shame, confusion, and helplessness; make their fears loom large; and challenge their worth. They defend their identity to a world they perceive as reducing them to their failures.

Because we do not want them fearful, pained, rejected, and disapproved, we proceed toward correction with overarching gentleness, kindness, and recognition of the load they carry. We notice how their opposition may mask fear, hurt, and loss, and avoid letting our objection to their behavior diminish our commitment to their well-being.

We correct their fear most reliably as we arrange a stream of successes at challenging tasks, a collection of victories. With that as their springboard, they look ahead to the next task and say, "I can do this too." Our success loop for them starts with practice that achieves a competence as quickly as possible. Teacher and peers then receive and affirm it and recurring practice makes it permanent. From direct experience, students perceive their environment as supportive rather than repressive and themselves as successful rather than inadequate.

To that context we add further themes here that touch more directly on order and cooperation. They proceed from inner to outer; from conditions internal to you as teacher, then to ideas you convey to students; and finally to conditions you apply to their behavior.

We discuss your own efficacy, the role of expectation, finding good in their behavior, the need for adult power, improving the odds of success, the benefit of indirection, asking their permission, the need for conscious agreements, the use of intense feedback, employing minor consequences, correcting the retribution principle, changing student thinking, an approach to a discipline issue, a note about pre-kinder behavior, and another about an independent kindergartner.

YOUR OWN EFFICACY

For many students an elusive moment marks a shift in their connection with you. Before it, they look past you, are guarded around you, comply minimally, and exhibit cues that they do not entirely buy into what you say. Then an event changes the atmosphere.

Perhaps you make an insightful comment toward them, provide them particular help, intervene to solve a problem they confront, are playful with them, or just speak person to person. After that they "see you." They respond faster to what you ask, have more positive feelings around you, and you can influence them more directly.

They still have problems and occasionally regress, but you recover lost ground faster. When something goes awry, you can return to your base with them, eye to eye with a respectful tone and calm presence, and resume your place in their world.

Impacting their thinking is the entire configuration of your mind, which you reveal through your personal relationship, that face to face you are significant to them, that you love them. You may give them a grade or a consequence, but if they do not bind to you as a person, many gains are foreclosed.

For this to occur, you accept comprehensive responsibility for them. To understand this, ask yourself, "To the extent that my classroom has a problem, how much of it is from circumstances *outside* me that happen *to* me?" Settle on a percentage. Now estimate how much you have allowed those influences to drain off your will to *determine* the order and learning in your classroom.

You might say, for instance, that the influences do not affect your motivation at all, or by 10 percent, or by half. If you are preoccupied with all the things parents should do for their children before they reach your class, maybe you conclude, "So then, it really isn't *my* responsibility."

Depending on conditions, your thinking may waver. When everything goes swimmingly, you feel in complete control. Outer influences appear to have no effect, but this may change sharply when students are distracted or uncooperative or when circumstances appear to neutralize what you attempt. In the moment it feels to you that others are the problem, and feelings of frustration or helplessness undermine your motivation.

It takes work on oneself to recognize that both students and staff simply manifest the stage of their development at any given time and that we must act in the real present. Your influence returns as you recognize their true state, perhaps modify an overestimate of their ability or yours, and adjust your actions accordingly. More is involved than just trying to solve a problem. An aspect of your own *actionability* was lost, so affecting others requires affecting yourself first. *We change something in ourselves to restore our responsibility for every condition we encounter.*

Few people appear to understand the causal force present in the secret, personal thoughts from which they devise their stance to the situation before them. The next examples offer clues to how far that causality extends.

THE ROLE OF EXPECTATION

Loving them. An eighth grade teacher was team teaching with a colleague. At a staff meeting one day he was informed that a woman teacher had referred to the two as elitist.

The teacher approached her and asked, "What do you mean by elitist?"

"Well," she said, "you must get *all* the good students. You *never* send anyone to the principal's office!"

At that, the teacher's colleague burst in, *"If you love them, you always know what to do!"*

Numbering the two of them among those needing no further instruction about this, the rest of us might look deeper. Influence arises initially from basic character, which the two exemplified, but much depends also on how we choose to express it. Note how those in the following examples asserted their beliefs and the effects that followed.

Respecting one thing. A building inspector often inspected the properties of a contractor who, he felt, continually cut corners. This set them up for constant opposition, so that a palpable negative tone persisted between them. The inspector wanted to change this and was intrigued by a suggestion: "If you can find *one* good thing about someone else, you can change *his or her* behavior."

He thought about it. What could it be? He could easily name ten things he did not like about the man, but it occurred to him that he genuinely admired that this man *knew how to make money*! He held onto that viewpoint the next time they met and noticed the atmosphere lighten. From then on, their relationship steadily improved until they greeted each other like old friends. The capstone for him came one day over one of the builder's properties where an undercutting stream threatened a hillside.

Unexpectedly, the contractor called him and said, "Come over and look at this!" Arriving at the site, the inspector saw that with a concrete truck and long hose, the builder had sprayed the entire hillside, solidifying it in place.

"What do you think of that?" he asked proudly.

"Yes, yes! That does it!" the inspector stammered. With good will, the builder had gone far beyond what was required in order to eliminate any possible problem. The start had been the inspector changing his own attitude, an internal gesture we can readily picture in a teacher: "I've tried being hard and angry and threatening to these students and it hasn't worked. Let's see. What can I *genuinely respect* about them?"

Being for them. A rural high school teacher drove a truck with a diesel engine and was returning home on a remote road after school when suddenly the engine died. He pulled over and was there a while when one of his students drove by, a boy he had severely disciplined that day. His heart sank, but the boy stopped, backed up to the teacher's truck, got out, opened the hood, diagnosed the problem, and fixed it.

The teacher was mystified. When the boy completed the work, the teacher was moved to ask him, "Why did you stop when I disciplined you so hard today?"

"I didn't feel you were *against* me," the boy answered.

Look in on that scene again and listen to the boy's words, " . . . *against me.*" How often have you seen teachers *against* students? With the contractor and inspector or with the student and teacher, once you get rid of opposition, good things can happen. The damage is not because you disagree with a student nor must discipline, nor by anything but your own attitude. The inspector's rule—*find one thing you can respect*—was enough for him to manage his own attitude and bring a new influence into play.

Back then to the teacher reconsidering her approach: "I know I've been against many of these kids. Somehow I need to pull *for* them and show that. How do I go about it?" Once she asks the right question, answers are likely to appear.

Holding the picture. The next incident moves a step further to asserting the highest belief you can.

A woman reported to her counselor that she was at her wit's end. A sociable and outgoing person, she was the sole secretary and office help of a professional engineer. Her problem was that he was extremely critical. Every day he had something negative to say about her work, and she was on the verge of quitting because it depressed her so. Since in all other ways it was a good job, she wanted to know anything she could do about it.

The counselor suggested one thing, that she *imagine* him praising her, smiling at her, and being warm and supportive, and that she hold on to that image no matter what.

Two weeks later she returned. For the first couple days when he would begin his criticism, she reported, she could feel herself slipping back into depressed and defensive feelings, but she resolutely maintained the image of him praising and supporting her. Little by little she noticed differences appearing, *and in two weeks his actions reversed completely* to match her image. She was delighted and glad to continue working for him.

The effect of the belief she sustained about her employer parallels the stunning finding of Rosenthal and Jacobsen in their landmark study recounted in *Pygmalion in the Classroom.*[1] It concluded that randomly selected students "bloomed" when their teachers were led to expect that they *would* bloom, regardless of whether they had previously done well or poorly — and sometimes even contrary to the teacher's conscious opinion of them. Once again we hear that the beliefs we act upon determine the experience we create.

We check in on our teacher's thought process: "Today I stop fussing and plant myself in good feelings, order, and cooperation as I change myself." The means become apparent only as the cast of mind is able to notice them.

FINDING GOOD

It may help you to view students' efforts more positively as you recall how artificial is the school setting. If you are bored, unchallenged, and have energy to spend, what do you do? The natural thing is to interact with others around you. Inborn needs drive you to reciprocity. You play, talk, wrestle, and let your mind wander. Remembering the drives fueling their growth, you might sympathize with the limits of the situation rather than blame them for failing to adhere to adult rules. The point is not to permit negative behavior but rather to begin by aligning your viewpoint with conditions as students experience them.

Applying a change presumes a basic connection with a student. Compare it to parenting. You would not manage your child's behavior only by random punishment. Even if consequences help you maintain order, an exchange with a child should first reclaim a solid bond between you—for the child a place of safety and well-being—and then you draw on it to resolve the issue. Reconnect and then communicate.

You probably do this already with "good" students. You like them. You talk to them easily, they respond when you speak, and they give you no problems. But what of the others who are not like that; who test you, ignore you, or breach your rules or values? How connected to them do you feel? If less so than with the others, *you need to work on yourself first.* Remove anything inside you that obstructs the outcome you want, any distance you yourself generate.

How to do that? How can you work around your own tendencies, and not allow their breaking of rules to affect your link with them? A simple equation is at stake: *The more students conceive you to be in opposition to them, the less you can help them change* (cf., also the section by the same title in *Effective Classroom Turnaround: Practice Makes Permanent*). Finding good helps us stay connected at a particularly decisive moment *when students expect us to be negative.* We must retain the ability to correct them in a way that they will not dismiss us, a way to continue to reach their thinking without alienating them.

We start with our choice of focus, *a la* the building inspector. *Find inside you a corner of respect for their capacities regardless of how they are used just now.* Once secure in such a feeling, we speak in an equal rather than imperious tone. As one adult asks another for information, we learn his or her side of the story. It should not startle us that other students and the teachers in that adult's life are not perfect either.

Presuming that adults already know we are positively inclined toward them, we ask a question implying that we expect the answer to make sense. Upon hearing their narrative of outer details, we invite the inner ones as well. Instead of saying *"Why* did you do that?" which they take both as an accusation and an invitation for an excuse, we ask *"How* were you thinking? Go back before the event. What were you thinking then? And what changed? And then?" Track their thoughts to find the point where a better course could be taken. "At that point, what would have worked better? What will work next time?"

Our concern is with the thought process generating the questionable behavior. In it is the material for an agreement about what they will do if the situation arises again. It should emerge organically from what they say rather than simply reflect our mandate. We do not want our ideas seen as imposed on them, but instead want them colored with a personal claim based on what they tell us. Maybe they tried to do something positive that turned out poorly and you can acknowledge it with a compliment at least for the intent.

Rooted in your respect for them, you may notice qualities you can mention specifically. Perhaps you appreciate their eye contact, attention to what you say, abilities you observe them use with friends, how they might put traits to use in the future or adapt them to good effect in the present. But just now, they have has used a strength negatively and you need to respond without losing your connection with them. You want to install a new viewpoint in the face of the misbehavior.

Four steps can sidestep opposition and free this adult from having to defend himself or herself while you offer a new viewpoint: Explain objectively 1) what their strength is, 2) its possible positive future use, 3) its current negative use, and 4) a better current use. Consider these examples:

1. Angela dominates a group discussion because she talks instantly after anyone else does. Strength: rapid access to words. Possible use: teaching, talk show host, getting along in public. Current use: cuts others off. Better use: wait for turn.
2. Calvin notices anything going wrong and criticizes it. Strength: insight into situations. Possible use: versatility in social affairs and business. Current use: introduces negative tone. Better use: notice what he can approve.
3. Don is reactive, taking others' comments as personal discounts. Strength: dignity, deep feelings. Possible future use: ease of belonging in a group. Current use: reactive at being discounted. Better current use: contentment with who you are.
4. Larry is a quick learner but interferes with others, sometimes upsetting them. Strength: ability to understand ideas quickly. Possible future use: mastering any field of knowledge. Current use: makes problems for others. Better current use: observe others' goals and think how to help if they invite help or leave them alone.

The outcome you want in each case is *a student's willingness to try a better use of a strength you acknowledge.* The fact that you speak objectively about it removes a possible barrier. The students need not prove anything to you because you already recognize more in them than they themselves might notice. You take a position on their side rather than opposing them.

Students who have a problem, will not work, or take teacher direction poorly respond often to a single lead for their thinking. If you can boil down a course of action into a simple, clear statement, they will often take it.

FIVE TOPICS

Just getting started with them may pose a challenge, but conversation even with nearly mute, withdrawn, defensive boys often opens up after they write out responses to five topics:

1. Things I am good at
2. Things that give me happiness and joy now or when I was younger
3. Things that have made me who I am
4. Things others see in me
5. Decisions I have made about myself

Examine their answers for choices they make, their opinion of themselves, and where their energy is headed. Identify an idea they can work to assimilate like "releasing down-on-myself feelings"; "focusing my attention," which is often helpful for ADD students who must do deliberately what others do spontaneously; "awareness of my will power"; "using words positively"; "how I affect others"; "keeping my hands to myself"; "growing up independent and on my own"; or "choosing my own direction instead of reacting to others." Often their answers to the first four questions serve mainly to heighten their general self-awareness. In that state, their answers to the fifth question can be extremely revealing, isolating the issues they can work on with teachers and counselors.

Tap into their inner world also by placing in front of them a list of feelings (cf., chapter 4 in this book or the appendix in *Effective Classroom Turnaround: Practice Makes Permanent*). Ask them to circle any they have felt in the last couple weeks, discuss the circumstances surrounding each one, and link them to their personal decisions.

ADAPTING TO THEIR NEED

Just providing them a solution-thought typically is not enough. Their unacceptable deed may be an acute phase of a chronic condition. They may, for instance, endure long periods of semi-invisibility, no one recognizing them as individuals, which drives either their effort to gain attention from adults or peers or a decision to accept isolation.

Unfortunately, our adult role may contribute by nudging us to attend to the impersonal progress of all, so we confine ourselves to measuring, criticizing, or approving that aspect. *For all it matters to our design of instruction, if someone feels invisible, we are okay with that.* We need to recognize this systemic conditioning and be ready to shift to the personal whenever we can.

Before school one day, a fifth grade girl slowly approaches a teacher to show him a black rock she picked up on the school ground that had not been there the day before. He thinks about it overnight, and the next morning when she slowly approaches him, he tells her that it was probably a meteorite: heavier than normal, black, and had undergone intense heat. As she gropes through her backpack, he expects to see the rock emerge, but instead she cautiously draws forth a trophy about the size of a baseball, inscribed "Third Place. Cross Country."

"Wonderful!" he says, changing tracks instantly. His mind had been on the universe and hers on "just me."

The idea we offer about changing their behavior must link to what is already there. In fact, we need their help *to adapt* an external requirement to their ongoing thinking, speaking as partners in problem solving: "Does this seem best for your next step?" or "Can you work with this idea for a few days?" or "Can you watch how this applies?"

Ask them to repeat the idea out loud and agree to try to apply it. A few seconds' attention to it early in the day may be enough to affirm it, and a few more at day's end to inquire, "How did it go? Does the idea still make sense? Does a modification suggest itself?" Note when they revert to floating and coasting and guide them to stay on track.

A fifth grade boy is pointed out as having a volatile temper. Staff admonishes him to no avail, so a counselor approaches and inquires if he would like a suggestion. The boy eagerly says yes, and the two quickly identify the issue as confined just to a half dozen students who made discounting comments to him.

After determining that he did not even want them as friends, the counselor points out that he could declare them invisible and let their comments pass by like the wind. When they approach him, he might look past them over their left ear *as though they were not even there.* A few days later the boy has a happy expression on his face, and the counselor asks if the method is working. The boy smiles broadly and says, "Great!" Sometimes their needs are very simple.

THE NEED FOR ADULT POWER

Your classroom can be a laboratory for helping students sort out unproductive attitudes. How they treat you as an authority, for one, is likely to foreshadow how they will regard superiors all their lives, so cleaning it up is a gift to them.

Your impact on them occurs within a spectrum. At one end you have no influence whatever, your words like a breeze that comes and goes while the student does as he or she wishes. At the other end you may sense your power to *crush* a student. You choose your point on the spectrum moment by moment, based on the need.

If the notion of using power toward students jars you, remember that many bear an unmet need about it and may present it to you full force—*a belief in their supremacy.* As long as they "get away with it," they have no reason to alter it. Urgently needing to know their limits, they learn this easiest as toddlers when a parent picks them up, saying, "No, you may not do that." They wail and struggle until they realize that adult power is greater and surrender to it.

If a child can evade this by complaining, protesting, begging, pouting, lying, etc., his cognitive mistake is likely to persist. If he thinks his power won, his illusion remains and his inadequate sense of limits may show up later when consequences matter more. Adults ruin the interface in two ways. They lose benevolence through turning hostile, blaming, or becoming uncomfortable, or they fail to maintain the confrontation until adult power wins.

Since teachers are limited in what they can do *in loco parentis,* our only available tack may be to give parents a handout. The worried and frustrated often seize eagerly any approach they might try. The steps below can affirm and extend what they do. Duplicate a supply and give one to any parent whose child exhibits oppositional behavior. Start it here:

1. Years ago, a psychiatrist named Martha Welch discovered to her dismay that her two sons were obnoxious. She had tried to raise them respectfully and kindly, but their attitudes had turned negative. Investigating the reason, she developed what became the title of her book, *Holding Time.*[2] In it, she explains a simple technique.
2. Pick an occasion when the child crosses a line of disobedience, verbal defiance, negative attitude, or noncooperation. Be prepared to spend substantial time. Twenty minutes may be enough but it can also take three hours.
3. Grasp the child firmly. Wrap your arms and legs around him/her as needed. Sit in an easy chair, or lie on a couch, bed, or carpet. Children may struggle to get away, but do not let them.
4. Remain kind and firm. Don't do this when you are angry. Think of yourself as a doctor applying a remedy to your child's needs. You are just carrying out the steps.
5. Hold the child for as long as it takes while you explain gently why you are setting a limit, the change needed in his or her thinking, how it will affect his or her life, how adults run things until children grow up, your care for the child, and so on. Flesh out a healthy, constructive viewpoint.
6. Your physical control delivers the crucial information that children are not the supreme managers of their life yet but are still under your power. You are their protector, and they need to respect your lead.
7. You will know you are done when your child relaxes, smiles, accepts your hold without struggle, and can describe to you what he or she understands you want. You might say, "Tell me what you're going to do differently now," and the child might answer, "When

you ask me to do something, I'll do it without complaining." Ask the child to describe how a specific behavior will change and the thought process he or she will employ.

Even one such experience can be a turning point for many children, while some need it a few times at most. Your intent, again, is to let them *experience your power as greater than theirs, change their thinking to accept that, and apply the change to their other behavior.* End the handout here.

Short of holding time, a teacher, principal, or parent can make the same point by remaining benevolent and doing the situational equivalent of holding them until they surrender to adult power. Parents concerned about their high school son's defiant attitudes "shut down his life": no fun, no phones, no TV, no friends. In a couple weeks he rethought his actions, made a change, and privileges slowly returned as he exhibited appropriate attitudes and behavior. We do children no favor when we allow them to evade limits.

Benevolence is important. We do not allow *their* behavior to affect *our* attitude. We do not let ourselves be manipulated, do not indulge our own upset feelings, but rather decide that even opposition or misbehavior cannot diminish the fundamental connection between us.

Use as your model the teacher to whom the student said, "I didn't feel you were against me." Apply sanctions *regretfully,* and never be vindictive, never take pleasure using power over students. We reclaim our relationship, exert the least intrusive impact that obtains the change, and proceed to the more severe only as we must. Many situations invite the following sequence that may occur in minutes:

1. Remove opposition from inside yourself.
2. Make eye contact.
3. Look longer.
4. Close distance.
5. Use their name respectfully.
6. Describe their unwanted behavior.
7. Correct the thinking that led to it.
8. Request an agreement about new behavior.
9. *Stay* until student agrees.
10. Apply follow up and consequences as needed.

If students protest a rule or argue the reason for it, explaining why may be useful. Even though you need not justify your actions to a student, you enlist group norms as your actions are thoughtful rather than arbitrary. Sometimes in both adult and student society "we do this because we have to," but this concession presumes a reasonable system overall. You might also seize upon a misbehavior as an occasion to take a student aside and have an in-depth conversation you have already thought through.

IMPROVING THE ODDS

To gain cooperation, think cause and effect. First ask, "What makes matters worse?" Figure it out—insulting, scolding, alienating, discarding, discounting, or oppressing—and at least avoid that. Then when you finally do hit on what helps, you have not dug a deeper hole to climb out of and your new intervention is more likely to work. Three points help you past the hole.

A manner of speaking. Let your words to students be firm but respectful—for a practical reason. When control is at stake, people instinctively notice any weakness in another's speech and take advantage of it. If a teacher's is not firm, students infer that *they* can set the boundaries. If it is not respectful, students take it as a discount, a reason for rebellion and distancing. We do not want any word from us to be an excuse for misbehavior.

Even in the adult world, differences alone may generate bad feelings. People think, "I don't like what you're doing," and illogically reason, "so I'm upset with you." Student attitudes that differ from the school's expectation invite conflict. We may feel that our role almost requires us to play out bad feelings. Another adult may *want* us to express them to validate their own, or they may seem the best way to declare how important the issue is to us. Our anger informs others how wrong they are, and we mount it to emphasize, "I really mean this."

Anger to deliver a message increases anger because students reinforce it by complying with it. Everyone assumes that anger gets results, so it becomes the ultimate hammer even if not expressed overtly. "They finally fell into line when I got mad," the teacher thinks, "so I have to be ready to show that," not noticing its residue of mistrust and alienation. For some teachers, their displeasure with students is their main message, yet they fail to recognize it as the reason their own day is reliably unhappy.

Clear, nonemotional directions work better. A parallel is a military unit on a parade ground where two words as signal accomplish "Right *face!*" Drivers advance with one signal, a traffic light changing from red to green. A consequence occurs if they do not, and knowing it is enough to guide their behavior.

Consequences should be objective and emotionally neutral, and the teacher even regretful about them. Applying rules impersonally, we step out of the loop. The issue is not that we exert power over them, but is only a relationship between them and the rule. We are fair and consistent because it is ingrained in humans and simians to protest what seems unfair.

Rapport. For students to think well with others, they need rapport—the realization that they match and are safe with each other. Cues they gather in microseconds tell them this—the tone and pitch of speech, words used, ideas offered, clothing, posture, and gesture. Common wisdom reflects it: "When in Rome, do as the Romans do."

Think of everyone you meet as "Rome" and you are visiting. To be accepted, do what they do, a theme especially useful for children. To help them join a group, tell them "Watch what the others are doing, and do the same thing." Their ability to blend with the behavior of their group largely determines their social acceptance.

A valuable understanding about this came from John Grinder and Richard Bandler as they developed Neuro-Linguistic Programming.[3] They sat in on sessions of the masters of psychotherapy, observing how they worked, and found one reason for their success in their rapport with clients. *By consciously adopting the qualities of the client, they entered their frame of reference* and could more easily exchange critical information enabling the client to change.

To apply this with your students, notice how you are different from them. Listen carefully to your voice. Does it match theirs or is it sometimes harsh? How would you like the sound of it directed at you all day? How often do you hear teacher tones around you that make you wince? Physical stance matters. Standing over them looking down conveys dominance while eye to eye expresses equality. Notice the pace of your respective movements, the arrangement of your posture and gestures, and the kinds of words you use. *They unconsciously code every discrepancy between you and them as a clue that they are less safe.*

As these accumulate, children conclude, "We're really different!" The more they see you that way, the less trustworthy and comfortable you appear. And when it is hard to see things the same way, cooperation is more challenging especially when you already expect a problem. Notice students' characteristics carefully and match them as you interact.

A common assumption can complicate this effort. If you believe that "students should adapt to *me,* instead of me to them," then rapport will seem irrelevant. But look at it this way. Once you offer a plan for learning, *everything else you do is just smoothing its pathway.* There is no point in making yourself a sandbar in their river. Adapt to them to retain access to their thinking and keep them moving ahead. If you increase their trust, you gain leverage to aid their learning.

When you try to obtain rapport by adopting a student's cues and want to know if you succeed, change your expression slightly such as by wrinkling your brow, tilting your head to one side, or nodding slightly. When they unconsciously imitate you, you are in rapport and can exchange ideas more productively.

Liking. All of us are oriented inside our own thought field. Since we perceive ourselves to be the master of it, we easily assume that our version of reality is correct. And being in charge, we expect others to fill roles in our scheme. The downside of our central place in our scheme is that it automatically diminishes our awareness of what appears at the periphery—typically, students' needs and feelings—yet *they* are the true scheme of things.

A way to counteract the automatic self-centralizing feature of our consciousness is liking students even if they misbehave. Once your own stance toward them is habitually positive, you can draw on your presence not as punishment but as focus: "Come here with me and just watch until you're ready to work." Be an emotional gas pump where they can refill their tank. Their internal world deserves at least as much care as how their behavior aligns with your rules.

When you have an emotional connection with students, your thoughts and feelings matter more to them. If their actions affect you, they may welcome knowing about it. Your cheer or anticipation about them can color their experience, but if you are a neutral figure to them, it makes no sense to inject it. *Especially while opening a relationship, be cautious about negative feelings you express toward them.* This formative time is especially vulnerable to casual discounts, and with some students, *you will never recover from them.* You want them instead noticing a substantial bond between you, perhaps even "when I'm an adult, my teacher and I will be friends."

BENEFIT OF INDIRECTION

A perennial behavior of teachers is *admonishing*—declaring an idea, rule, or demand students should follow that is laden with frustration because they have often delivered the point already without success. Learning, discipline, and classroom order are presented as requirements rather than as normal behavior: "This is what we do."

Control of consequences may manage most behavior but also leave untouched a deeper stratum of thinking that generates difficulties. When students notice we want them to think a certain way, *it may be harder for them to do so.* Teenagers often define themselves in contrast to us, raising a protective wall against what we propose. Do they want to let us in or not? To accept a good idea, they may almost have to forget it came from us. With their developmental task of gaining independence from adults, it can seem like their duty to resist us.

We sidestep this reaction as we build a perceptual field unobtrusively. Appreciation Time explained above does not *tell* students, "Do nice things for each other." It suggests it indirectly by asking, "Who was friendly toward you? Who was nice to you?" and then responding to their answer with a smile and thanks. Instead of ordering them to produce good feelings, which would be certain to fail, we merely draw their attention to them so they discover they enjoy giving them to others. They would rather follow out a discovery than comply with an order.

Our mandate for them to succeed at learning likewise falls flat after they hear it a dozen times. Instead, we ask them to stand, answer a question they have mastered, and be applauded. Their success at learning then feels that way, and they are more likely to master another piece the next day to reclaim the feeling. Applause supplies the conclusion we want but indirectly.

And when we ask them to rate themselves by the Perfect Conversation guidelines (cf., *Teaching Students to Work Harder and Enjoy It: Practice Makes Permanent*) or the Communication Skills Check Sheet (cf., *Effective Classroom Turnaround: Practice Makes Permanent*), they follow out the mechanics of the activity easily but in doing so notice better ways to manage their relationships.

Indirection never makes matters worse. We avoid trying to get something across to students just when they are determined not to listen. We do not risk our influence by overselling, but rather enable them to conclude ideas on their own. We arrange an easy activity that leaves an imprint behind.

ASK PERMISSION

Students live in two worlds. One we manage. We assign them places in it and apply consequences that make them feel better or worse.

Their other world is less accessible, internal to them, for their own use. They can comply with our outer demands yet live in an alien inner world rife with unproductive attitudes, feelings, and values. Guidelines essential for their lives may be poorly sorted out. Even if we use good methods to teach, students have the power to hold onto dysfunctional beliefs, so we need to gain access to their thinking even without any direct ability to modify it.

In this situation, advice from a spiritual teacher rings true: "When you are going to teach someone, do it humbly, like offering a gift to a king." "Humbly" means taking a lower position, not asserting our power. The idea of humility seldom surfaces in the annals of public education, but if we do not grasp it, we are sure to lose some of our students.

Notice why. The fact is *we do not control their inner world.* They are in charge of their consciousness, and we stand outside it. They can welcome or refuse our offering, can thwart what we want. We can choose to examine how our behavior could make us unwelcome or instead unadvisedly pound on the door of their mind, demanding entry. And in response they may decide startlingly early to screen us out, feeling unaccountably stronger doing so while we feel more frustrated. We may sense that this has occurred, abandon trying to affect their thinking, and resort to lobbing ideas at them with no assurance that they are welcome.

The step reconnecting us with them is *asking permission to change their viewpoint*. We knock on the door to beg admittance to the thinking that matters to them. "Permission-to-speak" acknowledges their management of their mind and that they can accept or reject our idea. Notice the courtesy and respect implied in the following lines:

- "Are you up for a challenging idea just now?"
- "Is this a good time?"
- "Is there a better time?"
- "Could I suggest a way you could solve a problem?"
- "When could we talk?"
- "What goal could we set for the next two days?"
- "Does this direction make sense to you?"
- "Jamal, I notice that you're working on X. Would you like an idea about it?"
- "Dominique, you seem to be running into the problem of X. Could we discuss it?"
- "Adrian, could we talk better if we waited till after school?"
- "Deena, would you rather work on this just with me or include your parents too?"

We *elicit* rather than command. They attend to something else just now, and our invitation implies that they will permit us to displace it. Standing as a petitioner outside their thinking, knowing they can dismiss what we say, we sensibly appreciate, admire, and fill our mind with their positive capabilities. We make it safe for them to open their thoughts with the assurance that they will not be squashed out of hand.

Teachers commonly *subscribe to* the idea of respecting students while not knowing how to demonstrate it. They may fail to notice how their words and actions deliver a contrary message. Anger and harsh words do not convey respect, and we do not reserve respect just for accomplishment. We do not accept or reject them by whether or not they succeed at tasks.

And if they clearly would rather not grant us permission to speak, we take time to think how to restore connection. Since their receptivity varies, we note when it is there. Think what you do when you do not invite another's idea but they launch it at you anyway. Even if it makes sense, you may feel impelled to refuse to let it in. *You knock on the door in a way that, if the answer is no, you are welcome to knock on it later.*

If they do not open the door, you 1) continue applying consequences fairly and objectively, 2) continue positive feedback to them about everything they do right, 3) think through the key idea you believe they need to grasp, 4) periodically but briefly mention it as it applies to their observed behavior, and 5) accept that for their own reasons they may keep you on the outside rather than the inside of their thinking.

We can offer such a respectful approach to their *ideas* even as we manage consequences intended to move their *behavior.*

THE NEED FOR CONSCIOUS AGREEMENTS

For many issues, we just clarify the action needed and obtain students' agreement to do it. Some classrooms benefit from simple guidelines discussed, agreed on, and reinforced, such as the following:

1. I pay attention when the teacher asks for it.
2. The teacher assigns the next task, and I try to do it.
3. I never hurt, insult, or discount anyone.
4. One person talks at a time, and others listen.

To assimilate such an agreement, students may need a couple weeks. They explicitly think about it early in the day, project an intention, and later ask themselves, "How did I do?" Someone—the teacher, other students, or their own self-report—needs to acknowledge and perhaps plot their gains. Without some form of checking later, an agreement alone seldom holds.

For making an individual agreement, do the following:

1. Boil it down to a single crisp sentence. "When X happens, I'll do Y."
2. Ask children of any age to look you in the eye and say it back to you verbatim.
3. *Have them repeat it until they can say it seamlessly.* Hesitations arise from parts of their mind that either have not assimilated it or still object to it. By stating an agreement congruently, unhesitatingly, and with appropriate eye contact, they enlist their conscious mind to give a valid command to their unconscious to carry it out.
4. Ask them later, "What was the agreement, again?" and have them repeat it perfectly.
5. Ask them to say it at periodic intervals until they can do so effortlessly.
6. Think through the physical actions leading up to the moment of keeping the agreement, and turn them into a Mental Movie you run several times with them. Many misbehaving students want to change their actions, but the part of their mind hearing the mandate does not inform the part reacting to the situation. You need to channel their imagery so they mesh idea and action in a continuous picture.
7. As with the agreement on classroom rules above, check later and give feedback so students realize their progress and can reaffirm their decisions that made it happen.

If students repeatedly fail to keep their agreements, a teacher may revert to ineffective scoldings, so it makes sense to diagnose the difficulty. Results improve as the agreement becomes more important to the student.

Assuming you have worked out content you agree on, what remains is its significance. Support for it lies in the consequences you, the school, or parents apply, and from the feeling tone of your interaction. For many students, peer attitudes weigh the most, so you may want to enlist the class. If you can rely on it to support you, call on it to help you convey to, for example, Kim the change needed. When he acts unacceptably, use the Consult so that the change you invite appears as a social act and not merely a surrender to you: "Maybe it can help you to know how others see this," or "Kim, you might want to know what happens to others when you do that."

Hear responses one by one: "Everyone, would you think of one word that went through your head when Kim did X?" or "What feeling came up for you right then?" or "What was your first thought?" Listen to a word or sentence from each and then discuss any theme expressed. The class might also tell Kim positive qualities they notice in him. The strengths others perceive are likely to be his resources for making changes.

Our problem with any student may be bigger than his agreement with us, however. He may not agree *with himself.* Any idea we pose may encounter an argument entirely inside him, manifested by his head shaking back and forth, a hesitant tone of voice, dropping certain words, mistaking their order, forgetting a key point, or equivocating by winks, grins, and pauses. Noting such cues, you ask him to repeat the agreement until it sounds firm, clear, and unhesitating from beginning to end, telling you that his subconscious mind has registered his intent.[4]

If an agreement is not kept, avoid the verbal constructions of *why* and *because* that invite excuses. "I did it because I forgot" may be taken as a legitimate reason: "We all forget sometimes, don't we?" But the word "because" is misplaced. The sentence really means, "I didn't care enough to make sure I remembered." In elaborating on reasons why he did it, a student looks *away from* his determination to change his behavior.

Rather, we focus on the shift needed in his internal self-talk: "What was in your mind *instead* of your choice to keep our agreement? How can we change that?"

While this may seem an easy task to an adult, school patterns can complicate it by continually breaking into students' attention. Their reality changes every time they change places. Subconsciously they may anchor an agreement to your presence and when you are out of sight, it may disappear. You may need to stretch it for them: "Now Kyle, we're friends here, right? And you do the things I ask and we get along fine, right? Okay. Am I still your friend when you go out to play?"

He may be puzzled about this but then realize that it is true. Similarly, "You love your mother and she loves you when you're at home, right? Do you still love your mother and does she still love you when you're here? It's the same with our agreements. We keep the agreement even when the other person is somewhere else."

Return to the theme often until you observe Kyle applying the reality of the agreement beyond your presence. The whole class can help you grade him 1, 2, or 3 for how well he kept it during recess or lunchtime, with applause as warranted. As children become old enough to sustain an intention, a grade given every half hour can be translated at home into proportional consequences of time at computer games or TV. Explicitly tying together deed and consequence can deliver a point even to children of limited understanding.

USE MINOR CONSEQUENCES

Small consequences for specific actions often help.

Field trip. Picture a field trip accompanied by two or three staff and/or parents who cross their fingers for good behavior. You might utilize them actively:

- Make a list of all students with a space for tallies next to each name.
- Ask an adult who knows all the students to maintain the list. Explain the expectations to the students. You will give them a signal for quiet when you want maximum self-control, such as a staff person's hand raised followed by five seconds during which they can finish their sentence and remind each other that their attention is requested.
- At random moments, the list-holder goes down it from top to bottom giving a tally to each student complying with the current expected behavior. He or she can stop at any time and resume from that point later so students never know when they might receive a tally.
- When a student requires a personal correction, the tallier marks an X, subtracting two or more plus-tallies from their score.
- By the end of the trip, everyone should have an equal number of chances to receive a tally. Students' totals separate them into those complying best, medium, and poorest.
- Grant a benefit to the first group, such as special activities, use of equipment, privileges at the school, or a movie. If all comply, all receive the bonus. The incentive would help calm most students' behavior.

These steps presume a specific type of labor, noticing *ongoing* positive behavior rather than the easier task of spotting *incidents* of negative behavior. *The principle involved is that what is noticed grows.* We want students knowing that we look actively for their positive behavior and intend to reward it.

Distraction time. To draw on time for leverage, use a stopwatch or kitchen timer to add up the length of all their classroom distractions for the day. Since they take up "your" time that way, you employ a logical consequence. You do the same to "their" time by carving it out of their lunch, recess, or dismissal: *Have them close their books, put away their materials, and sit silently for the total number of seconds they distracted the lesson throughout the day.*

With a class that is generally cooperative, such a penalty may be minimal, totaling only a couple minutes in all, but still feel molasses-slow to students. Even a little of it may be enough for them to urge each other to cooperate.

The small hammer. While most usually comply with rules, a few may violate them by repeated grabbing, pushing, ignoring direct requests, actions against school rules, or distracting others, and the school weighs whether to use a big, medium, or small hammer. We assume here a preference for the smallest that works.

We already improve the social/emotional skills of the group for their broad curative effect. Beyond that, *we quickly apply a specific consequence that students take personally.* Many will cooperate in designing one that affects them. They may want to change yet recognize that they do not have the willpower to do it alone, so they invite adults to place a sacrifice on them. Discuss what matters to them, which often lies in conditions that parents control. Motivating consequences they reveal may be loss of time for bike riding, video games, TV programs, friends, hobbies, or other energy outlets, or being confined to their room.

The best time to arrange consequences is before they are needed. When enrolling children or at the annual parent-teacher conference, obtain parents' agreement to apply them at home if warranted. Even if you think, "How could this sweet-faced lad *ever* misbehave?" discuss consequences when everyone is in good humor and settle on the best means of calling on them.

For one high school student heavily invested in video games, his homeroom teacher emailed his parents at the end of every school day. Five teachers gave him a score on a scale of 1–5; the last one averaged the total, and any score below a five brought on either a discussion and reprimand from parents or a reduction of his video game time, steadily improving his attitude and behavior over a few months. With a plan already in place, a quick email or phone call gives parents the information they need.

After-school time as a consequence should be possible either in your own room or with administrators. For the few who concern you most, you might keep an index card in your pocket for making tallies beside their name. Say to them objectively and neutrally, "For every occasion I need to ask you a second time to do something, you'll remain after school for one minute."

If they object that they cannot stay because their mother is picking them up, reassure them that you will invite their mother to join them. If they must catch a school bus, take the time off their recess or lunch, or accumulate it for a time when you can request the parent to stay with them at school. Increase the significance of the tally: "For any instances beyond three on one day, the time staying after school rises to three minutes for each tally." Find the level that affects them. Intensive checking and follow-up would not be feasible for every student at the same time, but usually intercepting a few instigators calms an entire class. Everyone realizes that boundaries apply.

When consequences do not appear to correct behavior, you may need to examine how students perceive the situation. Have they caught you in a game they believe they are winning? Teachers may think they apply a consequence, for instance, when they delay until everyone quiets down before beginning a fun activity. Yet even though students look forward to the new experience, they continue talking because it meets their need more directly than a delay in the next activity threatens it.

CHANGING STUDENT THINKING

Imagine that during playtime, one bonks another with a ruler and the other cries. At the behavioral level, the teacher intercepts the activity and draws on consequences and parental influence as needed, but our goal goes further.

A governing thought in the child *permitted* this to happen and may not be altered only by halting the problem behavior. In the child's mind, he may still believe that he was just playing, that he had a reason for what he did, or that is what people do. How many acts of violence has he seen in the media or in supposedly play conditions? Children accumulate a rich model.

The more decisive issue is *what does the child think about it*. You might view the problem as though an internal organ is ailing and a doctor needs to find which it is. We decipher the situation by accessing their mind:

1. If children feel upset, defensive, hurt, or angry, the feeling may hinder their clear thought, so you may wait a few minutes until they calm down. Sometimes just asking them to meet your eyes quietly for a few moments can change the track of their thinking. If you and they already converse easily, you usually need less time.
2. Frame the issue as mutual problem solving. With a matter-of-fact tone, say, "I'd like to help you solve that problem." If you ask

"Could we do that?" and they nod, they acknowledge a mutuality of interest. If no answer comes back, they may be so immersed in feelings that they cannot think straight.

3. Get a calm, objective description of the problem. You might say, "Okay then, fill me in on what happened." Get the facts straight: He said this, she did that. We set the stage with an expanded picture of the circumstances. This helps return the child's mind to where causality lies, bridging naturally to what remains unseen: "And what were you *thinking* when X happened? What do you think the other person was thinking?" We need to know how the child interprets the experience. What are his personal rules? What does he assume?

Talking with a defiant, monosyllabic, nine-year-old boy who could not put words to his feeling and was a puzzle to the staff, a certain look on his face suddenly informed the counselor. The boy had a marked sense of personal dignity and pride. From the teacher's action toward him he felt discounted, which spurred his inappropriate response.

The counselor explained his guess and the boy nodded slowly. Since the teacher's attitude toward him was fixed, the administrator tried a change of classroom and swiftly brought about cooperative behavior.

We connect circumstances to thought patterns: "I was only playing." "Okay, then. When you play, do you notice that some actions can hurt others?" What does he believe about force, hurting others, and accountability for others' well-being? How does he feel about reading signals of others' receptivity and how they view the situation? About "one thing leads to another"?

1. Avoid saying, "You *always* do X." It feels to them like a label pasted on them, as though they have permanently lost our respect. Instead we refer to the specifics that put the issue behind them. By defining what they have power to change now, we claim success for them when it occurs. "Remember yesterday afternoon when you did Y? I saw that. Good going!"
2. Upon identifying the key change in thinking needed, reframe it as their own resolution or agreement with you. They describe it back to you in words that tie it to its moment of use, repeating it piece by piece as needed. You give them feedback as they do it right:

- "When I play with someone and they ask me to stop, I agree to stop."
- "When I talk and someone ignores me, I can let it go."
- "When I have a problem with someone, I can solve it without getting mad."
- "When I want someone to play with me, I can ask them politely instead of grabbing or pulling them."

- "When I want to play, I'll remember the things that help me make friends."
- "When I want to make up a game, everyone needs to agree on the rules."
- "If someone pushes me, I'll get an adult instead of pushing back."

THE RETRIBUTION PRINCIPLE

Students' belief in retribution may need thoughtful attention: If someone hits you, hit back. If someone insults you, insult him or her back. Their playground actions may become the core of a model for how they think for a lifetime. All their lives they will run into *quid pro quo.* Given a negative *quo,* do we let them think that the *quid* they return should be negative too? "Do unto others *before* they do unto you" appeals to children at least as much as does the Golden Rule, and "What goes around comes around" may rationalize revenge. If they suspect they are being talked about, they readily assume the worst and act on it.

So a student does something to another and you would like to intercept him and engage his thinking differently:

1. Even one student becoming emotional is innately relevant to all. If the class was impacted by the event, use the Consult first. "What feeling came up in you when X happened?" "What was your first thought?" Students intuitively accept the collective reaction of other students as a ground of reality. As others comment, "When will they grow up?" or "That was immature!" or "It was just a downer," misbehavers are offered an alternative framework for their actions. You can hear from an entire class in a couple minutes, generating a vivid sense of their collective judgment. You can discuss their comments together or divide them into small groups, refer them to the Perfect Conversation or Communication Skills Check Sheet guidelines, and ask them to talk about their reactions to the event. Point out that this is not just to criticize anyone, but rather to become aware of themselves. What was stirred up in them, and what do they conclude from it?
2. Affirm the principle that applies. We apologize for hurting someone, we share, we take turns, we let others' ill-considered comments roll off us, we set things right if we injure someone, and so on. *We appeal to right thinking.* If they offered an insult, we want a change of attitude about it and invite a real apology rather than commanding it as a formality.
3. A principle that could alter many children's lives is "the first rule for getting along with people" (cf., *Teaching Students to Work Harder and Enjoy It: Practice Makes Permanent,* chapter 8). The rule is *to want*

the other to be happy and successful. It takes on most meaning when applied right when retribution is expected, so that they seek out ways to heal rather than hurt. It deserves periodic class discussion to help students realize how society has trained them to think in terms of conflict and opposition instead of the first rule. Discuss how using it affects their relationships.

4. Much in the social-emotional arena can be taught by having an experience and then debriefing the learning contained in it. To absorb the meaning in a moment of potential retribution, we express its immediate, relevant application in words. What impact did we notice? What did it imply for our life? What would we do or avoid? When students are willing to share such thoughts, we show them respect by referring to and building on their comments.

AN APPROACH TO A DISCIPLINE ISSUE

Sometimes we need to notice a student carefully and string together bits of accumulated information for what they tell us about his needs. A personal story: One day as I entered school grounds, I approached a small group. When I was a few feet away, an eighth grader with his back to me, whom I will call Kenny, said in a dismissive tone, "We're not ready for it, Dr. J.!"

Startled and lacking an immediate response, I ignored his comment, related briefly to the others, and went into the building. Kenny apparently expected a rebuke, and was warning me off. Another staff member who usually got along with him also caught a negative attitude. Kenny had arrived at school with a headband on, was asked to remove it, and resented the request.

Since he often projected that attitude, I wanted to try to reach him. Labeling his attitude unacceptable or offensive or punishing him for disrespect would not work. A consequence applied through his parents, who were prone to punishing, could make matters worse.

Later that day, happening to administer a state test to him in a quiet room, I pondered how to open the issue and settled on the least intrusive intervention, a behavior description. One describes an event neutrally and objectively, letting the other know only that the event had an impact and invited understanding.

As he rose to leave after the test, I said, "Kenny, could you wait a minute? I want to talk about what happened this morning." He nodded and sat down.

"This morning when I arrived," I said evenly, "I walked up to your group and you had some sharp words for me."

He launched into explaining. He had confronted the assistant principal over removing the headband, did not understand why this had to be, did not believe it was even school policy, and apparently expected me to scold him further. I explained to him why the school might have such a rule, which seemed to settle him for the moment but did not address his attitude. He still reserved the right to pop off when his eighth grade wisdom seized upon an offense.

A few days later during the day's closing discussion, I was offering one of my "Clues from Dr. John," this one about managing negatives in one's life (cf., *Teaching Students to Work Harder and Enjoy It: Practice Makes Permanent*). The approach suggested 1) recognizing when conditions stimulate negative feelings, 2) realizing that they represent weaknesses, and 3) immediately changing them back to correct actions and joyful feelings.

Students were taking turns reading a paragraph when an interruption outside the room caught the teacher's attention. When we resumed, I asked the reader to begin the paragraph again.

This upset Kenny, and he interrupted as though personally in charge. "No! We're not starting over," but we reread the remaining paragraphs, and the group was dismissed for the day.

A teachable moment opened. I blocked Kenny to prevent him from leaving. His behavior, I felt, tied directly to the point of our class discussion. Many of our attempts to guide students fail to lodge in the mental niche where they could be drawn upon. If one can use the impact of an event to convey an idea, it may have a better chance of being wired neurologically to the critical feeling.

"Kenny," I exclaimed, "do you think you have all of life figured out? Do you know all the answers?"

He looked down and shook his head. I wanted to enlist the part of his mind that knows he has much to learn while avoiding any discount, power contest, or arbitrary criticism. In the group, he had revealed part of his makeup we might examine.

"The impatience and irritation you felt a moment ago were *the point* of what we were talking about in the group," I continued mildly. "Things weren't going just the way you wanted. Well, that happens. In school, in life, in a job, in a family, things are always going to go differently than we want and feelings come up. Impatience and irritation are a weakness. If that's going to be your response to life, life will eat you up. You'll always be unhappy. If you're going to be a happy person, you need to master those feelings. Do you understand?"

His expression softened. From his nod, I gathered that he acknowledged my comment and might conceivably recall it later: *What you experience now is a weakness. Cherish the moment instead of fighting it. Use it to gain mastery over something in yourself.* Few students understand the type of effort involved in self-control, self-discipline, and channeling their emotions in positive directions. If we catch their emotions on the fly and spur them to rethink what they do, we may move them toward better choices.

PRE-KINDERGARTEN BEHAVIOR

A discipline issue in a pre-kindergarten class illustrates principles that can be used in several grades. Let us say that Jon in pre-kinder is pushing, shoving, poking, and grabbing so often that other parents complain. He seems impervious to corrections, and you suspect he may observe unhelpful modeling elsewhere. Following is my note to a teacher with such a student:

> I see a couple strengths to build on. The first is that he's responsive to you, wants your attention, and appears to want to please you. Also he wants to relate to others, wants to connect with them, but does it unproductively. Because of his age, he's too young just to hear an idea from an adult and convert it into behavior change, so we need to figure out how to use his response to you and desire for connection to alter his actions unobtrusively.
>
> First, doing Appreciation Time more than once a day might help, even for a couple minutes at a time. You might announce it after any period in which they relate to each other freely, such as right after lunch or recess. The starting question is, "Who was friendly to you today?" but we can build from there to help them notice others more distinctively, such as, "Who was happy today?" Jon could be recognized for being happy, for instance, even if he was not good at being friendly.
>
> Once accustomed to "friendly" and "happy," then "helpful" might fit after a classroom activity that makes it easy to share tools or materials. You can safely try out any trait you want to highlight: "Who was calm?" Shy kids would be glad to hear themselves described as "calm." "Who was kind?" "Who worked steadily?" The activity can acquaint them with an expanding assortment of positive behaviors.
>
> Beyond these more remote influences, the behaviors that concern you call for direct intervention also. I'd like to offer a picture that comes to mind. Our question is, "What could cause an idea to rise in significance to a child this young so he could actually use it?" The fact that he wants to please you and to connect to his peers offers a clue. Consider yourself like the conductor of a soloist and a chorus. You're sitting on the floor face to face with Jon. Ringed in a semicircle close around you both is the rest of the class, perhaps in two rows, shoulder to shoulder. A reason for arranging the scene this way is that you want Jon impressed with the feeling of being seen, so that everyone looking at him together represents in his mind his entire social world.
>
> After seating everyone this way, you say, "Children, we need to help Jon with something. Are you willing to do that? I'll tell you how in a moment, so listen carefully. I need you to be very quiet."
>
> Then say to him, "Jon, you come to school in the morning with a smile on your face (smile at him), and you answer questions, (nod affirmatively), and you . . . (tell him positive things you can say about him). And I know you like to play, and you like to play with other

children. Isn't that right?" Get a nod or agreement from him. Then say to him: "Sometimes children play in ways that don't work very well, and we need to find better ways. Remember earlier today when I asked everyone to form a line at the door?" Get a nod. "Do you remember grabbing Y from behind? Remember that?" Get a nod.

Then turn to the remainder of the class, and ask them to repeat after you, *"Jon, we like it better* (they repeat it phrase by phrase) *when you touch our hand* (for example, raising your hand and just meeting the other's palm) *than when you grab us."* After repeating this together in chunks, smooth it out so they can say the whole thing with you in one sentence. Show him how to meet your palm gently with his hand, and ask him, "Will that solve the problem? You touch hands rather than grab?" He may not even have noticed that there was a problem, so you've delivered both problem and solution at the same time.

You might not prefer to generate a lot of hand touching, but it can work to think of it as transitional. If the approach makes a positive change, you can also use it to modify the behavior later: "Let's think of ways we like others to greet us." From this beginning, you can address each of Jon's behaviors you want to change. Introduce the situation with positives toward him and a comment that "We want to keep improving the ways we play together" and "We're going to help Jon with something."

If you can, note a context in which the behavior you want to change is already positive. With poking, for instance: "Maybe you'd poke your dog to tickle him, but you wouldn't poke him if it made him angry or he wanted to run away, right?" Or about hitting: "Some people become boxers to show off how strong they are. But these things don't fit with us here, do they?" Then lead your chorus to say together to Jon, for example, *"We play better together when you talk to us."*

A common thread to many positive behaviors is the presence of agreement: *"We play better when you ask us first and we agree."* Conclude each separate issue by making sure Jon understands what the class is asking of him, can say it back in a clear sentence, and that he agrees to do it. At the end of each round, praise Jon and the class for "thinking together about how to help everyone be happy here at school." Keep a close eye on Jon, and give him early feedback: "During recess I saw that you kept your agreement, you did what you said you would do."

If Jon should happen to be so dazzled by all this attention that he appears to be screening it out, an alternate tack is to have the children line up in front of you and Jon. Have him do the hand touch with each child separately as they say the key request to him in a conversational voice. Hearing it eighteen times instead of once should deepen it. Individual contact and the group choral message together are likely to have a more telling impact than either alone.

A third approach aimed at conveying to each one that the whole group supports a student is "performing learning." Have a box of chips with each child's name on one. Think of everything you want them to learn in terms of a question they can pop to their feet and answer. The reason for standing up is that it makes the event more socially significant, more like a performance. While the child sits down, the class can applaud, communicating to them that their peers received their effort as worthy. This morning, for instance, in the story you read, I heard the hero theme, which invites questions to master, like "What does a hero do? A hero *helps people*. How does a hero help people? A hero *puts others first*." You might apply the latter nuance, in fact, to your perennial task of lining up to go places. Will they be heroes and put others first in line?

The walls of your room clearly have a lot of learning to deliver: "What letter comes after . . . M? N!" "What word starts with R? Robot!" Think of each Q and A as a little ceremony of its own that delivers the applause at the end. We want all of them to end the activity feeling that the approval of the group is significant so that they think in terms of behaviors that draw approval and that the group approves of them personally, easing their concerns about acceptance. The formality and consistency of the activity help convey these conclusions.

It increases the impact on students, I believe, if we tally on a chart each little chunk of learning they master and can deliver, but there's an organizing aspect to this that may be more effort than it's worth if other methods have the effect you want. If they don't, the added element of scoring (tallying) each thing learned and demonstrated would be my next suggestion. Included in what they learn could be a growing list of questions and answers about getting along with others, listening, learning, and following school rules.

Several days later, the teacher was excited at a reinforcement she tried. It was to look for "superkids" obeying the rules perfectly. When she observed a few doing this, she would take everyone outdoors to the adjacent playground and the superkids would play for a few minutes while the others sat and watched. She found she could time these mini-recesses so Jon steadily felt successful and within a week was more cooperative.

AN INDEPENDENT KINDERGARTNER

Following is a note to a kindergarten teacher coping with a student who a couple weeks before had been running independently down hallways as he pleased. The student had largely accommodated to the classroom but often did not do what the teacher asked.

Several subtle threads are involved, I think. The general aim is, "What does it take for adult influence to affect a child?" From the outside, it appears that you've established a positive learning atmosphere through a sense of order, clear directions, and moving their energy briskly from one thing to the next. Your leverage with them appears to come through firmness and clarity about what's acceptable and unacceptable.

My first guess is that the latter sometimes comes at a cost when you have to raise your voice and then show children your displeasure. Adults do this the world over, of course, and it usually works. The problem comes when a particular child, for a reason personal to them, doesn't automatically comply. A sense of opposition can develop that can create negative feedback loops. "I don't like what you're doing" comes across to the kid as "He doesn't like *me*." And the teacher sees the rule-breaking as "He doesn't respect me or the rules." Once defined this way, the situation is harder to turn around.

When we were standing at the door and you talked to me about liking him and how you considered the kids "yours," a smile creased your face that told me that's how you feel. When you were talking to him, however, you had a more severe look on your face that may have transmitted the message, "I'm unhappy with you." I think there are substitutes for both the look and the message and that the leverage for the situation lies in 1) you like him, 2) he esteems you, and 3) your personal presence impacts him. Here are the steps I'd suggest:

1. In your own mind, take a couple weeks in which your only intent for him is to *change his attitude* about complying with the class activity, that other tasks are just ways to practice doing that, and that the changes with which you accomplish that probably won't be needed for long.

2. Sit down when you can talk to him directly, so that your *eye levels* are about the same. Get him to face you, smile at him, and begin by just giving him feedback about specific things you observe that show he's growing up. "I noticed yesterday that X needed scissors and you saw that and handed them to her. It shows you're noticing other people." The intent of this is to let him know that you see him in a positive light and like him. Such comments can help him relax a little and know he won't be scolded.

3. Define the problem as *something you and he share* that you have to solve together. Say, "You and I need to solve a problem. I have a whole classroom to conduct, and the only way we can do that is when children do what I ask. You want to learn and have a good time at school. Is that right?" He should nod.

4. Define his *problem behavior in a constructive light*. This is important for removing the sense of opposition between you. Your basic respect for the problematic quality in him lets him know you haven't rejected him because of it. You might say, "Now I know you have an ability to *do things your own way*, and that's something you'll use your whole life. When you get older, you may be the one who thinks up a different way to solve a problem. So it's okay to do things your own way much of the time."

5. Note how *his use of the ability doesn't fit now*. Say, "The problem is, doing it your own way may not work when you're on a team. Then,

people have to do what the team is doing, or they lose the game, right? It's like you and I and everyone here are a team, and doing some things the same way helps everything run smoothly. Does that make sense to you?" He nods. "So would you repeat after me, 'I'm part of a team now'?"

6. Define his *lapses as forgetting rather than misbehaving*. It's true, in fact, that the proper behavior just wasn't in the actionable niche of his mind when he needed it, so that's the problem you and he focus on together. Say, "I know it's easy to forget the right thing to do." Defining it this way, again, removes opposition. Whatever you and he try is just a mutual attempt to "help him remember."

7. Use *expanding distance* from you as he becomes more reliable in acting properly at a distance. Say to him, "Let's have you and I stick close together today to see if that helps you remember what you need to do, okay?" Then as much as possible, keep him within arm's reach. When you have to be at a distance from him, check quietly: "I'm going across the room. Can you do (current task) on your own now for a while?" Resume close proximity, if possible, *before* any misbehavior starts. We want you able to say at the end of the day, "Hey, we did great, didn't we? Maybe tomorrow we can do even better." The next day "better" shows in his ability to conduct a requested task longer and at a further distance from you. You measure success, in other words, by the fittingness of his behavior as well as by how independently—distant from you—he can do it. His first success is to "do it great" sitting right beside you, and then a few feet away, and then moving across the room.

A final note. Your children may be completely accustomed to this, but dealing with many teachers and students, I notice variances in how they talk. You seem to speak quickly, I believe because you think and absorb ideas quickly yourself and also want to keep things moving in the class. In reconnecting with a student with whom we've somehow gotten onto different channels, this might be a starting point: Listen carefully to his pace, pitch, and tone of speech. For any ideas important for him to grasp, speak them to him with the same qualities his voice has, particularly when eye to eye and with that caring smile on your face.

SUMMARY

1. You must be a significant person to students.
2. Viewing them in a positive light has a powerful impact.
3. Finding a good even in their negative behavior places you on their side.
4. Students need to find a right relation to adult power.

5. You succeed better as you are firm and respectful, like them, and enter rapport with them.
6. Indirection never makes matters worse. Achieve goals subtly.
7. Ask their permission to engage in significant problem solving with them.
8. Make careful conscious agreements and follow up on them.
9. Occasional use of intense feedback from you and other students can help turn a corner.
10. Employ minor consequences accurately and reliably.
11. Correct students' thinking about retribution.
12. Over time, track a student's application of an idea you agree on.
13. Take total responsibility for every condition you encounter.
14. Find a corner of respect for students' capacities regardless of how they are used just now.
15. Explain to them their strength, its possible positive future use, current negative use, and a better current use.
16. To open students to dialog, have them write out things they are good at, that give them happiness and joy now or when they were younger, that made them who they are, and that others see in them, and decisions they have made about themselves.
17. The typical design of instruction is okay with children feeling invisible.
18. Parents may need holding time to overcome children's exaggerated sense of power.
19. What is noticed is what grows.
20. Apply quickly and objectively a specific, minimal consequence that students take personally.

NOTES

1. Robert Rosenthal and Lenore Jacobsen, *Pygmalion in the Classroom: Teacher Expectation and Pupils Intellectual Development* (New York: Holt, Rinehart and Winston, 1968 and New York: Irvington, 1992).

2. Martha G. Welch, *Holding Time: The Breakthrough Program for Happy Mothers and Loving, Self-Confident Children without Tantrums, Tugs-of-War, or Sibling Rivalry* (New York: Simon and Schuster, 1989).

3. John Grinder and Richard Bandler, *Frogs Into Princes* (Moab, Utah: Real People Press, 1973). This first book by the two authors is probably the most readable of their several valuable offerings explaining the main ideas of NLP. Many of its principles are salted throughout this book. Extensive entries in Wikipedia under each author can guide the reader through various avenues of development of their ideas.

4. Neuro-Linguistic Programming (NLP) is a fancy way of saying that we guide the mind through words we speak to it, an idea fundamental to good teaching that informs many of the approaches explained here. NLP has contributed an understanding of the depth and subtlety with which our words condition subsequent thought, feeling, and behavior. The idea that the brain reveals its assimilation of an idea by explicit cues is one such valuable principle.

NINE

Turn Around a Dysfunctional Class

Bring multiple influences to bear

Two weeks into the school year, a teacher of ninth grade students at a manual arts high school went on leave of absence.[1] His reasons bear careful thought because they reflect conditions that could worsen as shrinking budgets increase class sizes. Students did as they pleased, ignored his directions, and produced chaos. The principal gave him ineffective advice, security was absent, and his school has three times its design numbers. This describes a national problem: unacceptable behavior, resistant attitudes, unwieldy numbers, and ineffective support.

What could a teacher reasonably do in such a situation?

Typically we try one thing. When it fails to solve the problem, we drop it and try another. But a complex problem may not lend itself to a single solution. Instead we should expect multiple influences aligning. We retain the first one and add others until we have the result we want. We begin here with practical ways to bring the situation under control and then proceed to the more long term and developmental, drawing on several themes in the *Practice Makes Permanent* series.

Imagine that you teach in that district and are informed at noon on Friday that you will be transferred to the manual arts high school ninth grade drawing class on Monday. Where do you start?

A WEEKEND TO PREPARE

You hasten to the school's admin office, pick up a class list, and go through it with the assistant principal for a cursory take on each student and a look at their picture. You obtain parent or guardian phone numbers and plan to spend much of your weekend calling them. You want to talk with parents before meeting the students so that your relationship with them has priority. Later as you meet students, you want them thinking, "He knows my parents!" This alone nudges some to cooperate. Early contact with parents is important also because you can focus solely on positive expectations. You have nothing to complain about, no bad report to pass on.

Your message goes like this: "Hi Mr. Coleman. I'm the new drawing teacher for your son Corbin. I wanted to get acquainted with students' families a little since we did not have a chance to meet when school started. Could you tell me something about his interests and activities?"

You take detailed notes on each student, looking for motivating interests, best friend relationships, parent-child influence, and activities that might serve as disciplinary consequences. You might also ask if the parent has any concerns for their child they would like you to keep in mind, though their message could easily be, "Well, I hear that they ran off the previous teacher, so you may have your hands full."

In response you say, "I'm sure Corbin will do just fine in my class, but as a precaution, if something does come up that could use a minor consequence at home, do you think you could dock him time with TV, video games, or friends? We probably won't need to do that, but having it in reserve could be a help."

"Of course," most would say, giving conceptual assent to a plan you can return to in detail when you want to get Corbin's attention: "Mr. Coleman, remember that conversation we had a couple weeks ago? Right. Okay. Something's come up where we could apply that idea."

Arranging access is important. "One other thing," you add. "Often when something happens in the classroom, it can help if I can ring up a parent and have them talk to their child right then. Could I call you or Mrs. Coleman if that were needed?"

They already gave the school their contact phone for emergencies, and now you expand "emergency" a bit. Some you contact will be nonparental guardians who have little control over a student—a grandparent or older sibling perhaps—but you encourage them to remain connected to the student as best they can. You want contact, interest, and knowledge about the child supplying you with multiple handles for a personal relationship. Later you may draw on his older sister's explanation of his parents' divorce and how it affected him. You accumulate reasons *to insulate your own future attitude toward the student* from one of opposition to one of support and earnest problem solving.

Another task for the weekend is to obtain a two-foot by three-foot tablet from the school, ideally with one-inch lines already printed across each page, and make up several charts. Early Monday at the school resource room, cover them with acetate for easy erasing. One has all student names down the left side and nine wide columns occupying the space to the right. A couple you fill with row and column lines, covering them entirely with one-inch squares. These will be line charts. Another has all their names down the left and one-inch row and column lines filling the space to the right.

OPENING THE DAY

On the first day, stand at the door outside the classroom and have students line up. Admitted one by one, have them tell you their name, shake hands, turn to your notes for that student, and check all the positive information you already know while you connect it with their face: "Ah, yes. Mr. Billings . . . parents Jane and Joe. Did I write down their phone number correctly? Thank you. And Mr. Percy . . . has a younger brother and sister. Thank you." You want to learn their names as quickly as possible, let them know that you see them as individuals, and start off warmly.

Relating to them this way is important because misbehavior accelerates as students think "Everyone is doing it." It diminishes as they think, "Uh, oh. The teacher sees *me* doing it" — a minor but helpful recasting. In their perceptual field, consequences are cushioned by their solidarity with a group. Their individual behavior does not seem significant even though they dimly foresee being called to account for it. If they are punished, they know they will still be with their friends. You want personal accountability to you stronger in their mind than group support for unacceptable behavior.

The price of obtaining this is your effort to establish a relationship with each one individually. You want a connection with each student tight enough that you can restore it even in unsettling conditions just by approaching, saying their name, catching their eye, and asking for the behavior you want. They think afresh about their link with you as you possess personal data about them right at the start, pose no threat or opposition, and have direct access to their parents. Others around them may get in trouble, but you provide them an avenue to exempt themselves if they choose to use it.

Early on, *try to arrange their cooperation* without them even realizing it. You are like a salesman whose objective is "the next yes," like the car salesman who encountered a customer one morning and showed him a car. He began talking *and continued for eight hours without stopping* until the customer bought the car. He presented one idea easy to accept. A string of such ideas wound through more and more issues, resolving each in turn, until with the final yes the customer agreed to purchase. In class, you want a string of yeses that gradually return them to learning by aiming for one easy agreement after another.

At first they are still embedded in their social world. Too jarring a request, too big a leap, and you disconnect. They turn guarded. Suddenly they can more easily say no than yes and sense that you will ask them to make shifts too abruptly, stretch their cooperation too far. A saying attributed to Stalin applies: "If you're going to steal a salami, do it slice by slice." You identify where they are but, with one simple step at a time, lead them toward cooperation.

While many opening gambits might serve, the Consult referred to earlier has many uses. You ask a question to which everyone has a personal, brief, relevant answer, and hear them all quickly. You might say to your new class, "Occasionally, just to check out how you're doing, I'll ask you a question that invites an answer from everyone. Right now, are you feeling up, down, or in the middle? Let's start over here and go around. Jason, are you feeling up, down, or in the middle? If you want to answer with a hand signal, you can do that too."

The hand signal costs them little effort and is personally relevant, brief, and easy. They can even give a thumbs down just to hint to you that they are in no mood to be trifled with. Yet thumbs down signals comprise minimal cooperation you can draw further with another easy yes. Again, you remain *inside* their frame of reference, offering no abrupt shift that might derail cooperation.

"Hmm. Several have given a thumbs-down signals," you say. "I'm sorry about that. When people aren't feeling good, it can be harder to learn. Isn't that your experience?" You nod and watch them. You might engage a little more eye contact as several nod along with you. You continue:

"Let's hear what the down feeling is about. It's different if you were angry at someone even before you came to school, versus being sad or worried about something. If we can, we'd like to lay those feelings to rest before we start into learning."

Note the embedded suggestion: "We're going to solve a problem, and then we'll get down to learning." Two vital assumptions are voiced as though accepted by all. Remaining inside their perceptual field, you focus on the more personalized material that warrants deeper attention:

> Could we go around again, and this time give a specific feeling word to your inner experience, like sad, loss, angry, worried, or whatever fits? If you're feeling good, try to put a word to it—interested, happy, anticipating, grateful, or whatever. You're the only one who knows what you feel, and no one is going to correct you about your feeling.

Listen carefully to what they say, and notice what might warrant follow-up, maybe someone's personal experience to talk out right then. Stand closer to the student expressing the feeling—we'll call her Jessica—and say to everyone, "These kinds of feelings can really get in the way," and then to her, "Jessica, would you like to tell us what made you sad?" Hear the story. If you notice a spontaneous response in others, invite it out. "Anyone like to say anything to Jessica? One at a time please. Okay, Arianna?"

For many problematic feelings, a general tactic is to ask the class, "Think when you or others have felt like that. What kinds of things do people do to get past that feeling?" An unhappy feeling invites problem solving *about the feeling.* Solving the problem the feeling concerns is a different matter that may not be accessible to your influence, but Jessica's current feeling may hinder learning. It lies inside her, was brought into the room, she offered it vocally for a collective response, and now it is available for surgery.

The invitation to the class to tell how they (or someone) might handle such a feeling may or may not uncover a solution a speaker can adopt directly. More important is that asking the question *implies that such things are to be handled*—not coddled, claimed as one's identity, exaggerated, nor dramatized. You tell them gently that "people handle feelings." Also, other students' comments to one student imply personal connection: "I've been in your shoes. I know what you're feeling. I want to get through this with you." The process hints at camaraderie, acceptance, and understanding.

You go around to another student. Alan may doubledown on his feeling, and grumpily say to the class, "None of those things would work." What do you say?

You tell the truth while assuming a constructive course of action: "Thanks to you all for your help. One person's solution may not work for someone else. Sometimes we can only offer clues for the others to think about and arrange in their own way."

The message to Alan is, "You're going to sift through these clues and come up with your own solution." You may take him aside later with your own suggestion: "Alan, I thought of something that might help." On subsequent days, observing an altered affect in him, you ask, "So Alan, has anything changed for you about that issue? Did a new angle come up for you?"

Learning about emotionally significant material often works best when stretched out in time. Episodes may provoke a deep reaction, but long-term change may involve an intricate interplay of information, perception, choice, and action. Ideas that start the process may be offered briefly at first. Then students notice how they apply to their ongoing experience. They modify their thoughts or actions a little and return to class with a slightly different stance.

Your daily attention *just plants a single piece a little deeper,* knowing you can return to it on subsequent days for watering and pruning. If an early discussion takes ten minutes for them to grasp one good idea worth follow-up, this is a high-value use of time. As their attitudes and behavior turn positive and cooperative, the time needed diminishes, leaving them better able to concentrate on learning with less transition time.

The Consult can be used any time an event occurs that impacts everyone. In a chaotic classroom, from their body position and expression, you can tell that the experience variously generates distress, worry, disgust, or excitement. With the Consult, you help return them to basic group norms: "Could we hear a word from everyone on what they're feeling about what just happened?" Likely, they will offer a sprinkling of "boring," "lame," or "When will they grow up?" letting perpetrators hear thin class support for their behavior.

ENGAGE PERSONAL OWNERSHIP

Turn to the charts you prepared and posted on the wall, and explain how you plan to use them:

> When you go out for a sport, you want to know how you're doing, how your effort helps you improve, so you collect your statistics, your "stats," if you can. Knowing the result of your effort helps you figure out what to change. Scoring adds interest. If you're playing a game and someone says, "Let's just play and not keep score," the game usually becomes less interesting, right?

Notice your appeal to the easy yes. You are about to ask them to do something familiar. They keep score constantly, but you bend the practice slightly to aid learning.

"This chart has all your names down the side," you say, pointing. Instantly every one of them scans the chart to locate their own name. Whatever you say about the chart has just increased in significance.

> It's about concentrating. Beside your name are columns, each with a date on it. At the end of each day, I'll give you time to multiply two things, the number of minutes you concentrated on your work times your degree of concentration 1 to 100. Think of it as minutes times a percent. So perfect concentration — not a single distractive thought — for 50 minutes means 50 times 100 percent, or 5,000 Concentration Units (CUs). If you fool around most of the period or let yourself be distracted, you might multiply 20 minutes times 40 percent concentration totaling 800 CUs. Every day, enter a figure in that day's column. At the end of your row is a space for a cumulative, running total of your CUs. If I think you either overestimate or underestimate your concentration, I may mention it and we can compare notes. The number you give yourself isn't graded but is just a tool to help you keep track of your effort.

That a chart contains each student's name and is displayed publicly is not lost on students. They cannot resist comparing the score they claim with what everyone else enters, and they will know if anyone exaggerates their score. To increase the relevance of the measure, you might discuss their perception of their ability to concentrate—what helps, what hurts, how to think about it, how to apply it, and the difference it could make for them. You could tell them about Albert Einstein, who claimed to be able to work without a single distractive thought for forty-two minutes. You continue:

> The next chart that's blank now and has no names on it will be a line chart for the class overall. I'll fill it out for you based on a slip of paper you give me at the end of the period that answers two questions: "How did people treat me?" and "How did I treat them?" Just write "I'm treated" with a number beside it, and "I treat" with another number beside it. A 10 means really well, and 1 means poorly. I'll average the numbers you turn in for each category and post the "Am treated" line with a blue marker, and "I treat" line with a red marker. These two side by side let you see how you view what you do overall. If the two lines are very close together, this would mean that everyone is really being honest, facing what they do personally, and acknowledging others' positive actions accurately.

The chart becomes significant because *just measuring a behavior implies a direction for improvement.* Students like to regard themselves as getting better at anything socially valued. Few issues are more important to them than how others treat them, but you want them also noticing the correlation between what they dish out and what they receive. You might gather the same data also by asking them literally to count up the number of positive actions of others toward them, and the number they themselves do toward others.

When they are accustomed to the measures above, present next the chart containing nine wide columns with their names down the left. At the time you draw it, leave enough margin at the top so that on a slanted line at the head of each column you print titles as follows, large enough to be read from anywhere in the room: 1) look at speaker, 2) leave brief silence (explain this as "Don't interrupt"), 3) speak in short messages instead of long speeches, 4) ask a question (peer to peer), 5) connect ideas, 6) summarize others' ideas, 7) give compliments, 8) include everyone, and 9) tell what helped you. Post the chart where it is accessible both to you and the students.

Each of these behaviors is observable. Learn them well enough that you readily spot students doing them, and at random moments, go to the chart and make a tally in the appropriate column beside the name of a student who used a skill. Catch them in the act of doing the right thing *without even asking for it.* The "yes" is so easy that they have already done it.

A teacher used this in a class of high school students all so dysfunctional they had been expelled from public schools. Quickly they became interested in the teacher's tallies. At first they treated it as a joke, but then became more serious and invested in it. When she was focused on other matters and forgot to use the chart, they reminded her. She then allowed them periodically to go to the chart and give each other tallies for behaviors they observed, steadily improving their communications and relationships.

You can use the skills in many ways. You might brainstorm with them a list of topics they would like to discuss and rank them in the order they prefer. Then give them just eight to twelve minutes a day in groups of three or four to talk about a selected issue using the skills list. Afterward they go to the chart and give each other tallies for the skills they noticed being used or do this verbally as they conclude the group. While extended discussion about topics can be valuable, our more elementary aim here is *establishing group norms for high quality communication.* With these in place, a host of desirable results becomes achievable.

With the dominant group norm tilting toward consideration for each other, Appreciation Time is a simple but powerful way to deepen those feelings and reinforce constructive behavior. Ask each student in turn, "Who gave you a good feeling today and what did they do?" They answer by naming another person and telling what they did. The student speaking is reinforced for recognizing the deed, and the other for doing it. As the question is repeatedly asked and answered, they realize that friendly, constructive behavior gets attention and inconsiderateness and unkindness appeal less and less.

OPPOSITIONAL STUDENTS

Given a reasonable outlet for positive energy, most students will use the opportunity. These slowly become your allies as you call on their perspective with the Consult, welcome their good feelings with Appreciation Time, record their feedback with communication skill tallies, and make their academic effort successful. A common perspective develops in which students think, "It's better now," "I feel safer," "We're treating each other good," and so on.

Still, a few may retain attitudes that buck the desired trend. You may already know who they are because *they rankle.* Something about them gets under your skin. You may observe gratuitous, unprovoked inconsiderateness toward others or deliberate interference with your attempts to teach and cannot pin down what they think.

A guess is that many of these students *have an exaggerated sense of their own importance.* Along with idiosyncratic qualities arising from their personal experience, they somehow chose the common solution of declaring themselves above and beyond others' control. They may show it in evasive ways such as lying, avoiding, delaying, and passive-aggressive behavior, but also more assertively by interrupting, insulting, disobeying, ridiculing, bullying, ignoring common rules, and criticizing. Often they carry their maladaptive attitude into their adult lives, perhaps disguised, yet resulting in slow sabotage to their progress.

The issue is important enough to bring principal, counselor, teacher, and parents to the same table. While adults' urgency may focus on ameliorating specific conflicts, a central attitude change is the long-term issue. Together adults need to find a way to convince the student that he or she is not in charge. For those still physically manageable by their parents, Martha Welch's book *Holding Time* is a valuable resource, explaining how, by holding a child, you can reinstruct them in the appropriate parent-child power relationship (cf., chapter 8).

For the ninth grader who already weighs 210 pounds, an alternative is *to shut down his life until he gets the message.* He has *no* independent time, *no* video games, *no* TV, *no* time with friends. At school, he becomes the assistant principal's new sidekick, stands and watches while others have recess or free time, eats lunch alone or with adults. School staff and parents must be in harmony about the urgency of this direction: *This child has a life-destroying disability, and we must exert maximum effort right now to turn it around.* Yes, it inconveniences everyone, but that also is appropriate. Until now, *everyone failed* at getting this message into his head when doing so could have been easy.

If you made your initial contact with parents as suggested above, this follow-up will be received well. Parents typically experience frustration similar to the teacher's, and now you are their ally, helping to figure out how to give this child a new direction.

YOUR PERSONAL RELATIONSHIP WITH STUDENTS

The activities noted above may seem alien to you for one reason or another but are listed first because you can choose to do them quickly. If they are so incongruent that you could not see yourself doing them, we might look deeper not at your students but at yourself. Our first concern is your belief system, which we referred to in chapter 3 (cf., note 7).

In sum, back in the 1960s, a study by the University of Florida asked entering college freshmen to identify their best and worst K–12 teachers. Those named were approached and invited to participate in a study about teaching, with the intent of finding out what made them different. These were not your general spectrum of ability but were *unanimously* named best or worst; yet almost all measures the study applied did not distinguish between them. They appeared to know and do about the same things. The startling difference was in *their belief system.* On some twenty dimensions, poor teachers had negative beliefs where good teachers had positive ones about self, students, the world, and the teaching task.

This poses a strong hint to a teacher trying to change a student who is already negative. Every negative label you add has a depressive impact on him independent of your actions. Your behavior may be approximately the same as a great teacher's, but students know your heart. If it is frustrated, angry, depressed, helpless, or indifferent toward them, you need a way to change it. Your attitude will be the first force they encounter when they enter your classroom.

You may regard this facet of your makeup as set in stone. "I am who I am," some say, "and don't try to change me." If you are convinced that you have to be negative *and do not want anyone to talk you out of it,* then you should probably find a job where you do not deal with people. We assume that your students innately are not the most cooperative and that issues arise continually, and you need a way to deal with them that sidesteps conflict. What could it be? If you would like to modify your belief system, here is a way to go about it.

The solution is to recognize *in their misbehavior itself* something you can respect. Sharp tongue? He's got a feel for words. Interrupts? Wants to participate. Laid back? Easy to get along with. Takes over everyone else? Potential leader. Slow to participate? Wants to get things right.

For anything students do, they use a capability. Distinguish it from its current misuse, make clear to them the part that you respect and appreciate, and help them recognize how to use it more constructively. You are frank about the good, the potential, the capacity you see, and now the only challenge is making it fit the situation. In that frame of mind, you are better able to develop a stream of positive things to say about any student so they grasp quickly that you are on their side.

PURSUE AN IDEA

To work toward a connection with a recalcitrant student, set a time when you can talk with no pressure. Ask him or her to write out things 1) I've enjoyed now or when I was younger, 2) I'm good at, 3) that made me who I am, 4) that others see in me, and 5) decisions I have made about myself. You may come upon startling leads to discuss: "Kids think I'm mean" or "I'm good at embarrassing others." Their skills and interests often open conversation about current activities or aspirations for later. You let them know you are personally interested in them, and gather content for positive comments you can offer later. Every day there should be some way you see them in a favorable light even if connected to something that did not go well.

This personal knowledge and your ease of exchange with them make it feasible to introduce a thought for them to ponder: "I notice something that might be useful to you. Could we talk about it after school? Or how about tomorrow morning?" Where possible, give them a say over whether and when you will talk. If they are in a defensive, depressed posture, be more explicit asking permission: "It looks like something is weighing on you. Could we talk sometime this week when it fits your schedule?"

You approach them as having power at least equal to yours in the matter, but in fact they have *decisive* power over whether or not even to let you in, which they determine solely by how you treat them. Talk out the issue and aim for an agreement in one sentence: "Would this work: 'When those kids show up, I just quietly go somewhere else' or 'Whenever I'm upset, I remember I can calm my feelings' or 'My attention will wander forever unless I take charge of it'?" Write out the agreement for them to post on their wall at home.

Soon afterward, ask "What was our agreement again?" and every couple days ask "How's the idea working?" Reaffirm what it was, get it smooth and complete in their mind, and encourage and praise its application.

USE MINOR CONSEQUENCES

You need minor consequences that bite just enough so students want to avoid them, but not severe enough to upset anyone if they endure them. A careful accounting of distraction time matched exactly by consequence time often serves the need.

It presumes that methods like those above have corralled the main energy of the class, but students may still burn up time in getting down to work, verbal distractions, gratuitous comments, rising from their seats and moving around, and urgencies they feel they must resolve with friends. Prepare by obtaining a kitchen timer graduated in seconds. A wall clock with a sweep second hand can work, but takes more attention tallying individual times on an index card or a scrap of paper. Explain ahead what you are going to do and then carry it out reliably:

> We appear to be taking time in distractions that eat into learning. To remind everyone, I'll raise this timer, say 'Your attention please,' and count up five seconds for you to return to your seat, finish your sentence, or end whatever off-task thing you're doing. Then I'll start the timer and stop it when the distraction ends and you're ready for the current task. Through the day (or period) I'll continue adding up all the distraction time on the timer. Then we'll devise ways to spend exactly that amount as consequence time, such as staying here after the bell, returning at the end of school, or some other consequence we can discuss.

Maintain a gamelike tone, light but impersonal. If you yourself are upset about their behavior, *you place yourself in opposition to them.* Think of it rather as a minor problem you help them solve.

Students respond well just to subtracting distraction time directly from recess, lunch, or afternoon dismissal. Have them sit silently in the classroom with books closed and no conversation, watching the clock for the specified time. Even a couple minutes of this may be uncomfortable enough for many to change their behavior the next day. It directly impinges on their freedom right when they are poised to be off and running with high-value time.

You might also offer them bonus time for periods of substantial learning and cooperation, and subtract the distraction time from their bonus time. As they accumulate the latter, you and they together can choose games, a movie, or other feasible rewards they might enjoy.

Some will object that only a few distract the class. Your preference however is to ask *the class* to bring them in line. "If some are distracting, it affects everyone's concentration, so just remind people about what they're doing." You want them buying into a group norm and applying it to each other. Absent that cooperation, you can apply accurate record-keeping and consequences for the few.

HAVE SOCIAL SUCCESS BY LEARNING

Aim to align their basic work at learning with their social needs. You provide them a way to experience competence and have peers recognize it. This elementary model drives all the games they play that are not sheer chance, and it is the intuitive measure they use as they present themselves to each other: "I'm on top of this, and I want you to acknowledge that." We can help them meet this need through learning by the following steps:

1. Whatever you teach them that has cognitive content (i.e., even drawings have cognitive content), frame it as question and answer.
2. Have them write out a complete, comprehensive answer so they can learn it perfectly. They *need* to learn to write in order to be competent adults, so don't short-change this essential step in order to "go faster." Make sure everyone understands everything and has it written down.
3. Assign them partner pairs to practice explaining it so they both know it. This step brings their personal learning into a social arena. They are stimulated by the expectation of another student facing them to whom they must try to make sense and want to feel that they have risen to the challenge presented. They have the complete

written answer before them, and now facing a peer who asks them the question, they are set up for success.

4. They practice it back and forth until they can both verify that *their partner* knows it and, as time allows, retrieve answers back to the beginning of the term.

5. You deepen social relevance by arranging performances. Write out all questions on separate slips and drop them in a bag. Every day or two, for a few minutes, draw a slip and a name. The student stands and performs the answer, and everyone applauds.

Partner practice consolidates the learning, performing it deepens their claim on it, and applause is probably the strongest form of peer recognition. You can also count up all the questions they learn and post these growing numbers on a wall chart.

ORGANIZATION GROUPS

Students are anxious to be accepted by their peers, so an easy yes is to offer to organize them in small groups with their friends. The process can help you penetrate the hidden layers of influence among them and enlist the strongest students as allies.

Ask everyone to take out a sheet of paper and draw a line down the middle. Each student writes his or her name at the top, "Who would I like to be in group with?" above the left column, and "Who could I best learn from?" on the right. The first question taps friendliness and the second respect, but both predict, "Who will I cooperate with and allow to influence me?"

Explain to them that you are going to make up groups and will try to arrange them as best you can with others they want to be with. Ask them not to share their nominations with others. Only you will see the slips they turn in, and assure them that they can name as many as they want. Before they turn their paper in, ask them to check that their name is written at the top so you can tell who nominates whom.

Two issues are critical for the success of the groups. One is where to place students who relate poorly to others, are on the social margins of the group, and are most likely to be rejected. The other concerns student leaders who could help you shape the attitude of the class. To compile the information you need, sit down with all the slips that students turn in. On a large piece of paper, make up a chart with both *a row and a column* named for each student. Take one student's list at a time, go to his or her row, make a tally mark in the column of each other student he or she names, and do that with all the slips turned in.

The result is a visual picture of students' liking for each other. Those most named—with the most tallies in their column—are the most influential and are your group leaders. Those naming each other are good friends. Those least named overall are the students who most need careful placement and support. Begin your group assignments with the latter, *giving them their top picks,* particularly if they chose influential students who chose them in return. As you assign those remaining, check their selections against your own knowledge of those who do not get along or who lead others into trouble.

Try to form the most support *around* the students least socially connected, aiming for a group size of four or five. The former is ideal for conducting partner practice within the group. Having three potential partners offers a mix of stability and variety. If any students have an early problem in their group, try to adjust quickly but move stronger students rather than those least named. The latter have already had their share of rejections, and moving them is more of the same.

Take aside your most-named group leaders, *and in every way you can, run the class through them.* They first help their group pick a group name. Then make them responsible for conveying, collecting, and accounting for assignments. Instead of making announcements and instructions to the class yourself, meet with your group leaders, pass the word to them, they pass it on to their group, and they lead their group's cooperation.

Have them plot learning and concentration stats as a group. Do performances of learning a group at a time. Make them responsible for supplies for their group, monitor their group's behavior, and round them up after a recess. Get group members thinking "we" in all ways you can, and the leaders thinking "my" group. Appreciate their effort, and point out ways they can help their group with issues of attitude, behavior, and learning. Consult with them over any issues arising with their group members.

Most classes can probably be influenced with less than the complete array of activities described above. For a significant change in students' thinking, however, we are more likely to succeed as we engage multiple influences that nudge their energy into a common channel.

SUMMARY

1. Classroom management may become harder as shrinking school budgets increase class sizes.
2. Multiple influences are likely to be needed to turn a class around.
3. Obtain comprehensive knowledge about students and direct contact with their parents.
4. Set up agreements with parents about later use of consequences.
5. Collaborate with a student in problem solving.
6. Make up charts for scoring a variety of classroom conditions.
7. Meet and greet students personally.

8. Strong individual bonds with students help you draw them one by one from poor behavior.
9. Arrange for them to cooperate without them realizing it.
10. Plan to achieve your objectives by a stream of requests, each easy to agree to.
11. Use the Consult to check their collective mood and identify key issues to discuss together.
12. Help them process unwanted feelings constructively.
13. Invite them to estimate and chart their concentration level hour by hour.
14. Invite them to estimate and chart how well they treated others and others treated them.
15. Measuring a behavior implies a direction for improvement.
16. Tally their use of communication skills.
17. Use Appreciation Time daily.
18. For oppositional students, create the consequences that impact them sufficiently.
19. Your belief system is a powerful tool.
20. Help students change by tracking a single, personal idea redirecting their energy.
21. Use minor consequences barely uncomfortable.
22. Have them master learning by explaining it to a partner, scoring it, posting it quantitatively, and performing it.
23. Enlist the most influential students as group leaders, and run the classroom through them.

NOTE

1. Sandy Banks, "At Manual Arts High, A Caring Teacher Is at the End of His Rope," *Los Angeles Times,* Sept. 24, 2011, and also, Walt Gardner, "A Teacher's Worst Nightmare," *Edweek,* Sept. 27, 2011.

TEN

Hone Your Viewpoint

Key zones for teacher intent

The focus of this book is first about you, about what you will do, and only later about your school or external limitations. They are circumstances toward which you direct effort. Teachers next door may be fractious and uncooperative, your principal preoccupied, your students ill-mannered, and your state requirements unreasonable. As onerous as those conditions may seem, they still leave you still a rich field within which to design your strategy.

Others who care about you will understand the stresses on you, so consider exploring with them the surges in your stomach, heart, and throat that signal concerns to work out. Try to help each other through the burdens and responsibilities you face and together form a plan for action. Here I propose eight abilities to practice that could enhance your effectiveness:

1. *Notice students.* See the classroom through their eyes and intuit what they think and feel. That expression on a student's face—what does it say about his feeling? Their body position—are they all tired out? The quiet murmurs you hear—do they fit the task or are they headed toward distraction? The head lowered and the impassive face—is he carrying a special load today? Use your eyes and ears to assemble accurate data about them and their needs.[1]

Your success depends on this. No matter how clever the methods at your disposal, only your grasp of their thoughts and feelings just now tells you the direction needed. For the task to flow smoothly, you have to notice and remove the glitches. A certain unselfishness is presumed. What becomes important is not your own thought or feeling but their

137

involvement with learning. You speak sparingly, enough to orient them and arrange the task that fits next.

2. *Maintain their full attention.* Many teachers do not appreciate the difference between what they could accomplish with students' full attention versus with driblets and do not know how to obtain the former. A high school student described how his teachers would arrive charged up about an idea, and students would think "Oh boy!" But after a ten-minute presentation, they were done, and the remaining time became aimless or boring.

Engaging their full attention requires a channel, one step leading to another that feels to them like progress toward mastery. They keenly recognize whether their effort is directed or left to wander. It inevitably will unless you know what to ask of it.

The steps explained here meet this need. Each engages their energy, moves them toward conscious mastery, and all can do them. Patterns of activity once understood, such as obtaining hard copy and partnering, can start off in seconds instead of in distracted minutes. Students are glad to adopt the patterns because they realize they genuinely learn.

3. *Sustain positive direction.* Guiding ourselves depends on a constructive direction of thought. Many accept this in principle but are easily jarred from it by trying circumstances just when they need it most. *Focus on what you want rather than on what you do not want.* A true story illustrates.

A man was urged to visit a great aunt staying at a home for seniors. She was so negative that people could not stand to be around her as she poured out endless complaints and criticisms, so he decided to try a strategy suggested to him. From whatever she said, he would ask a question about the least negative part. Hearing her answer, he would again ask a question about the least negative part, and so on.

Following this plan, he quickly initiated a long and pleasant conversation with the aunt, but a later effect was even more striking. Those with whom she stayed reported that she was in a good mood for three or four days afterward.

This is focusing on what you want. If he had said to her, "Auntie, everyone says about you that you complain and criticize all the time. Why do you do that?"

"Obviously," she thinks at once, "it's because everyone else is a stupid dolt," and she continues the cycle. His comment reactivates her negative pattern.

Apply this to a distressed school staff. A new principal declares, "Everyone says you're bitterly divided and call each other names. This is a bad idea." The comment re-energizes the history. Without an effective means of turning it around, the comment makes matters worse. From whatever its starting point, the strategy needs instead to take a constructive direction and sustain it, which is the point of the techniques explained above. The trick lies in dealing with negativity in a manner that transforms it, beginning with mastering one's own reactions.

In response to a question, a teacher of fifth graders proposes two words as simple life goals, to be *imperturbable* and *impeccable*. The first is to refuse to allow any external thing to shake their emotional balance and remove them from their best thoughts and feelings. Negative effects are certain to occur unless they do this. The Latin root of the second is *peccare*, meaning "to sin." In all their endeavors, they aim to be flawless, to do it right, to maintain their own highest thought and action.

4. *Release reactivity.* Everyone has better and worse traits. Any of us may note a weakness, reconsider it, and shift to using a strength, a redirection lying close to the heart of personal change. We seize control of our inner world. Common experience offers reminders: "Come to your senses," "Let it go," "Take it easy." We decompress one sensation and replace it with a better.

In a sense, human nature can be thought of as mechanical or conscious. Driven by the first quality, we react to circumstances as preprogrammed. Propelled by a sensation, we catastrophize, "make a mountain out of a molehill."

Searching instead for conscious activity, we resist a reaction in order to weigh the best response, asserting mastery of our inner and outer actions. Our conscious positive process begins as we cease reacting to what is outside and choose from what we have inside. *We begin our quest for good feelings by deautomatizing our response* so that we can truly seek out the best one.

Ideally, if we were moved solely by logic like Spock or Data in the *Star Trek* series, we could work out problems directly. But instead, feelings leap to the fore: "This isn't what I want." We react and attach powerful emotions to what we lack. Recycling the thought *"Not what I want"* generates hurt, anger, fear, guilt, timidity, disappointment, and their many cousins. We sustain the feeling and its conclusion by steadily returning to the sense of lack as though driven by an operatic chorus. A thought-stream may collect all sorts of negative feelings that injure us further, even paralyze our progress. Settling upon *lack* as our state, we conclude that we deserve to be upset.

5. *Remove the sense of lack.* A remedy lies in making peace with reality. Whatever it is right now, we say, "Yes." We accept its existence the way it is. Paradoxically, this restores to us the power to alter it and dismiss negative feelings, a principle with a distinguished lineage. Saints of all religions advise us that detachment is essential to a spiritual consciousness. When we are not detached, the world jerks us about.

We need not cease having intentions and goals, but rather stop investing our perception of momentary lack with negative feelings. Understand the problem. It may be true that we do not have something. It is not all in our head. We really do not possess this item, but we can seize on that fact as the supreme value of the moment and lather it with intense feelings and great importance.

Instead of struggle with what we do not have, we move toward full awareness and acceptance of the reality that *is* there for all its potential and learning. We allow our minds to welcome in the riches of the universe and of our own consciousness, place ourselves calmly in them, and from that stance deal with the issue before us. We dismiss tension, insecurity, and worry about controlling our world, and turn our energy instead to drinking in awareness of reality. There, our capacity to choose emerges clean and available in our consciousness, and we discover that we can act differently about the need.

We are first truthful: "So there's the problem. Okay. To work on it, *I release the charge on it.*" We do not violate our rationality by denying its existence, but we also notice that our emotions apply an unneeded force. If we can discard it, in what remains we are more rational, balanced, and able to respond.

This principle can change our lives and teaching. When ideas jar us, unpalatable memories intrude, or other people dismiss our thinking, we must relinquish our reaction in order to grasp what is offered to us. This is elementary self-correction: "I want my best thinking. My emotion blocks it, so I release my emotion." Inquire of students often, "Is this your best thinking?" Many teachers reinforce this instinctively: "Thank you, Conrad. That was a *good choice.*"

A critical route to our own good thinking is allowing others to challenge us on its quality. We need to welcome it when they do so and thank them, and—the graduate level—take it to heart when they finger our attitude as the real culprit.

6. Meet emotional needs. Remember a time when you felt that the world was a dismal place. How long did it take you to work your way out of it? And did you do so by yourself, or did others help shoehorn you past it? Now think of students constructing a world-view while feeling depressed, criticized, and anxious. Their needs for attention, acceptance, approval, and affection are so strong that failing to meet them can interfere with their ability to think.

Even with ten minutes a day to address feelings, you are likely to have a more productive class. We want students to know that good feelings can predominate in their lives, that they can generate them and construct a happy world. A certain assertive skill is involved. Situations can cast us unwittingly into unfamiliar emotions or into repeating negative ones we experienced in similar situations before. We recall whether the time was happy or not, challenging and stimulating or not, satisfying or not, and our prior mood transfers to our new setting.

Recall a subject you learned while you were unhappy and how your feelings affected your interest. Was it harder later to pick up the subject because it returned you to your previous feelings? If you are bored when you learn social studies, you conclude that social studies are boring. Feeling and thought feed each other. A pessimistic feeling carries the thought, "Things probably won't work out." An anxious one declares, "I'll probably fail." A hurt one reminds us that "people don't like me."

The link between feeling and idea challenges us not just to change a classroom's atmosphere but to redirect its thought processes. When students associate good feelings *with being with these people,* the feelings attach also to what they are doing.

7. *Bring out the best idea.* It is not by accident that successful people distinguish themselves. They think differently. They are better at bringing the best idea to the need of the moment, at not letting their mood, a temporary feeling, an intrusive thought, or a defensive reaction derail them.

Much depends on remaining preoccupied with what one needs to know. Upon assigning a task to our mind, we discard thoughts of a negative tone because they diminish the productivity of our thinking. Bob Proctor, author of books on business success, commented one day that he had become incapable of negative thinking because he had trained himself in that regard for so long. A sense of lack, frustration, or struggle typically poses a barrier to fulfilling our goal.

Your cast of mind is central to the step you select. Even competent people may find themselves in a funk. Someone may worry or upset you, a work situation challenge you, or a health issue preoccupy you. Your cat's abscessed tooth may bother you as much as it does him. You hash over things partly beyond your control.

How you do this, the viewpoint you bring to it, affects you. Intruding into the edges of your thought and draining away its finer qualities may be your images of when a problem got worse instead of better, when you failed or looked bad before others, occasions of embarrassment, patterns of self-blame, or injuries to your self-esteem. All these line up at the edge of your consciousness to exclaim, *"See? It's happening again!"* You find yourself fighting off fearful thinking.

A better process is to face a challenge with curiosity about what you will learn and fascination at the steps you might take. Pose a random thought and add, "I wonder what . . ." Notice how different it feels to be curious and fascinated instead of worried. You reconnect with occasions when you noticed and thought well, acted to achieve a goal, and met your personal standards.

From there, you scan your responses. Where before you may have been negative, you instead search out your best resources and are more alert to ideas afloat around you—and from out of that alertness, choose what to do in the classroom. You take the time to sort out better and worse in your thinking, apply the better, and improve at it by practice.

8. *Expect students to work.* A certain helpful attitude might be called "the Straight Nail Principle." One envisions a pioneer father putting a

hammer in his son's hand and directing him to pound nails, but the boy does not hit the nail squarely at first. His glancing blows may tilt a defenseless 8-penny nail this way and that as the father watches. With the son about to give up, the father says, "Hit it again!"

About nails and most things, you have to hit them straight and then keep at it. You have to understand the effort called for and apply it precisely, making better results instantaneous. Hit squarely, the nail goes in every time.

The principle operates with a student having trouble with an assignment. He has looked at it this way and that and still does not get it. There is no natural limit to the mistakes possible, so he could go on endlessly until he stumbles upon the key. But with a single comment properly directing him, he proceeds.

From being scattered and ineffective to being on target, how long did the change take him? *Just one moment* in which he got the focus correct. The change happened immediately when his attention was properly directed. Let students know the effort that matters, then their action is effective, they take off in smoke, and you can turn your attention elsewhere.

Children do not do well with the time-lag adults accept for success. Remember your children's first step and first word. Were they not instant successes? Effort this minute should mean success this minute, effort today means success today, and success means a claim on satisfaction and social approval. People want to know that their effort gets them somewhere.

Success is not the only value, of course, and they will need to learn that failure can be valuable and success delayed. But we have to know what we're doing. Effort can be boring and pointless or energizing and inspirational depending on what we arrange.

The endpoint of a student's effort for each piece of learning is just having conscious, mental control of it. Even first graders can learn a simple lesson completely this week, reaching the pedagogical endpoint of continuous, conscious mastery; owning a piece of knowledge, knowing what they know.

Yet our ultimate purpose extends further. By student effort, the accumulation of knowledge continues without limit, with no end point. Varying the means and pace of this can help stimulate students, but *the work is theirs.* Do you like it better when you work hard and students work a little? Or when they work hard and you work a little?

If you use a little of your effort to pinpoint exactly where their effort gets the best payoff, it turns out that you work little, they work much, and their work is highly productive. *Your understanding of where to direct their attention is the key.* Only your insight guides them to the activity having the highest payoff.

And what activity is that?

The answer every moment depends on the quality of your thinking. You attend to the intangible issues that affect the class; understand their thinking, feeling, and assimilation of their current chunk of knowledge, and the best step to move it forward. To think this way, you need your own mind as clear as possible.

You are like a winning coach noticing every detail of a team's effort and outlining its next step. You work a little at comprehending their path of growth, and they work a lot at the activities moving them along it. You dream the plan, and they carry it out. You sleep on it, and they work like Trojans the next day.

SUMMARY

1. Notice students. See the classroom through their eyes and intuit what they think and feel.
2. Maintain their full attention.
3. Focus on what you want rather than on what you do not want.
4. Release reactivity. Slow down and manage deliberately your automatic responses.
5. Remove the sense of lack. Make peace with reality, accepting its existence as it is.
6. Face problems with fascination instead of worry.
7. Determine to meet students' emotional needs.
8. Bring out the best ideas.
9. Arrange for students to work steadily in a way leading to permanent knowledge.
10. Your understanding of where to direct their attention is the key.
11. Changing alone is very difficult. Most of us need support.

NOTE

1. Another useful and urgent idea from NLP is sensory acuity. You must observe conditions in the world outside you in order to understand the effect of your actions. If you refer only to your preconceived assumptions or habits of thought to gauge what you do, you inevitably generate unsatisfactory outcomes that you blame on the world outside you. Ideological fixation can displace sensory acuity in education planners.

ELEVEN

Know What You Are Doing

Grasp the difficulties of change

YOU YOURSELF OBSTRUCT CHANGE

That you have read this far is welcome, yet you are not likely to apply the ideas in this book. *Not even if they improve what you do, are easy to do, and solve problems you face.* Few of us are really free to change substantially by ourselves. You may be one of them, but probably you need people on either side supporting you, possibly a supervisor directing you or a government entity ordering you and then rewarding you for complying. Why should this be?

The difficulty is in human nature, that each of us is extremely narrow. Personality is a sort of hypnotic trance where symbols, impressions, and guesses compete toe to toe with truths. A collective script grips all of us, making it hard for us to think apart from our reference group. Our attention is driven daily by our assumptive world, and we miss countless great ideas because they fall outside our prior thinking. Even people acknowledged to be open sustain only a limited field of understanding, and it may be hard for them to stretch beyond it.

And now you. To be honest, could we say that you basically have your mind made up on all major issues? Our personal fund of knowledge deposits us inside a stance to every human experience. Once we claim an identity and world view, altering even a single aspect of it faces built-in resistance. Because our thinking determines our results, when results do not change, we can reason back that our thinking has not either. Your classroom remaining the same raises a mirror. You also are the same and will not be able to transform your classroom or school until you think differently.

This is not to say you do anything wrong. A certain effective teacher steadily looks for the extra mile he can go to help students. He would not limit his thinking from any ungenerous impulse but by already having a classroom, a pattern of life, values that engage him, and activities consuming him morning until night. Because his mind is filled, another would find it hard even to suggest that he could multiply his outcomes with different methods. Old good ideas hamper new good ideas.

BEGINNER'S MIND

The ability to relinquish an old idea and adopt a better one is often referred to as *beginner's mind,* remaining teachable. In truth it can be extremely hard to obtain. For us to add a single thing to our lives, it must take over a niche already claimed by something else. New information may contradict opinions we have long harbored, or we may need to acknowledge that we believed something incorrect or that our former actions were counter-productive. We instinctively avoid such thinking because it undermines our confidence that we are rational and competent. We resist the idea that we could awaken one morning to note that the person in the mirror is not acting as we expected.[1] How come?

Too many issues of the day seem held in place by educators *committed to what they do now,* not on principle for a good reason, but from habit and the self-reinforcing momentum of behavior. Such a pattern is apparently not limited just to conversations about education. Although a saving remnant in society dedicates itself to the discovery of truth, society at large competes instead over *what to assert.* The game is how far to push the envelope. Assimilating ideas just because they are true has less cachet, so that education planners instead apply a presumption: *We decision-makers with our power to control students and teachers are going to require them to do this.*

Creativity with other people's lives is the great social game. We take up an impression, pose our idea against others', and see which wins — forgetting that each is only an impression we can leverage far beyond its value. Any field may harbor a paralyzing mindset. "It's difficult to convince nonsense that it is nonsense," said William Gladstone. An editorial writer noted, "It's hard to get someone to understand something when their salary depends on them not understanding it."

Once one's own assertion or turf is valued more than truth, *there is no logical stopping point.* Nothing in nature spontaneously brings our own assertiveness into balance. Instead we wait for our very mistakes themselves to cave in upon us, with the country's financial debacle beginning in 2008 a painful example.

A contrasting stance might be: How are teachers and students *doing*? What is the truth of their experience, and how can we guide it toward the greatest well-being and success? We first grasp what is there and recognize how it limits what we can assert. Maybe the amazing advances of the last couple centuries have left us presuming that reality can be taken for granted—*we know all that, right?* So therefore we do not have to figure out how reality works and live in accord with it.

FIXITY OF SCHOOL DESIGN

Fixity of thinking can express itself in the design of schools. Sometimes an unexpected clue gives us a corner-of-the-eye glimpse of the determination with which we channel our thinking. In the 1960s, for example, shortly after the Soviets shocked the world by rocketing Sputnik into Earth orbit, many wondered what Soviet education might teach us. Royce Van Norman wrote then in the *Phi Delta Kappan:*

> Is it not ironic that in a planned society of controlled workers given compulsory assignments, where religious expression is suppressed, the press controlled, and all media of communication censored, where a puppet government is encouraged but denied any real authority, where great attention is given to efficiency and character reports, and attendance at cultural assemblies is mandatory, where it is avowed that all will be administered to each according to his needs and performance required from each according to his abilities, and where those who flee are tracked down, returned, and punished for trying to escape—in short in the milieu of the typical large American secondary school—we attempt to teach "the democratic system"?[2]

Did that speed by too quickly? Did you get it? *In the milieu of the typical large American secondary school* delivering the impersonal control of students? That is where much energy goes, an effect perhaps even stronger now than in the 1960s as the School-to-Prison Pipeline expands in scope. You may wish to transform your classroom or school, yet shadowed by prior efforts that have gone awry, do you understand that you tangle with failure?

Although you undoubtedly are intelligent, your reason for failure is likely to be that intelligent people can run their behavior with mediocre thinking.

MEDIOCRE THINKING

A consultant once explained the problems million-dollar Internet companies run into.[3] The main difficulty is that people do not identify and overcome their single main limitation. In some aspect of their business, their thinking is mediocre and they accept it out of habit.

Three clues point to it. One is expending a great deal of effort and getting little back. When the main limitation is overcome, typically the reverse happens. A little effort brings great results.

A second clue is that people fix on their potential—an attractive opportunity, a personal skill, or an unusual resource. Because it excites them and feeds their hope, they preoccupy themselves with it, and get even better at what they already do well. But if actual productivity is stalemated, the problem is not with the potential and the block must be elsewhere.

A third clue is that people stuck in problematic thinking may already be told the answer. Others around them see their flaw clearly and tell them so, but they fail to listen.

Apply these clues to your school system. Lots of effort for minimal results? Probably true. Great potential everyone agrees on? Certainly true. Choruses of people hammering at the flaws in the system? True again. Conclusion: Is it time to check the influence of mediocre thinking?

It may soften our resistance and open us to receiving challenges gracefully if we keep in mind how easy it is for large numbers of even smart people to make big mistakes. Recent instances have affected all of our lives. Assimilating what was already known could have prevented disastrous outcomes:

Vietnam War. Big thinkers assumed that because their perceived enemy was evidently an ally of China, they did not need to talk to the North Vietnamese. They thought they already knew everything they needed to know. *Big mistake!*

The Wall Street 2008–2009 Meltdown. Mediocre thinking about risk, deregulation, and social responsibility dominated. *Big mistake!*

The Iraq War. Mediocre thinking weighed the need for the war. *Big mistake!*

General Motors. Mediocre thinking, reversed only long after by government intervention after near-disaster, weighed markets, fuel efficiency, and supply and demand. People screamed at them to take a different course, but they would not change. *Big mistake!*

Gulf Oil Spill. BP oil company cut corners repeatedly, not concerned that things could go awry. *Big mistake!*

The lesson of these examples has broad application. If we are not accomplishing our goals, we first check *ourselves.* "My school isn't achieving its objectives *and therefore I think incorrectly.*" Does that ring true? You may object that you are not the one responsible, but every human has agency to use as he or she will. How do you use yours? Do you set mutual goals with others affected and pursue them?

We may come up against flaws and irrationality, but we can choose to address them effectively or mistakenly. Doing the latter sabotages our efforts. Social patterning and lazy ideas seat us on a bandwagon heading over a cliff. If we fail in our classroom and school, the most likely reason will be our own mediocre thinking.

THE LARGER MEANING

Rationality presumes seeing the larger meaning. Events occur in an elusive field that invites our insight. We need to recognize when we are about to operate by knee-jerk response. If we fix on one annoying condition, we lose track of broader values. Xerxes, who became king of Persia in 485 B.C., had a servant whisper in his ear every evening, "Remember the Athenians" and became obsessed with a vast, unnecessary military operation that marked the decline of the Persian civilization. For you and me, does a black figure in our mind's eye represent our own Athenians?

Larger meanings envelop us, begging us to decipher them and think rationally. Those in state government affect education directly. Early 2009 saw a research study that inquired how Arizona should cope with a projected budget shortfall. Ninety-three percent said that the best thing was to cut state spending while less than a third preferred to raise taxes. Researchers then asked what people wanted in the seven biggest budget items beginning with schools. Sixty-three percent wanted *more* for them.

Comparing those who wanted more versus less spending for the other categories, the first group was larger for *six of seven budget areas* with prisons and corrections the sole exception.[4] People declare loudly, "Cut spending." Then as though changing the subject, they say, "Spend more on my priorities." This is not rational, but it is common. Mediocre thinking believes it can both cut spending overall and increase individual programs.

This matters to our discussion because *the quality of thinking in schools mirrors the quality of thinking in society.* When the latter is irrational, it can drive out rationality wherever the two touch, so that schools, like society, may only erratically seek out evidence, be logically consistent, and make sense overall. We are spurred to notice whether we do any of the following:

- Fail to obtain evidence
- Overrate evidence supporting what we want
- Underrate evidence contradicting what we want
- Place undue emotion on pros and cons
- Rely on habit

ALTERING MEDIOCRE THINKING

To protect you from yourself, *pounce on* whatever does not make sense to you in your own actions and change it before it sabotages you. You may have better luck working with a team, leaning on others through the discomfort of change. Instead of having troubles assault you and force you into a new direction, head them off early. Sensible people assess evidence and make changes before driven to do it.

Invite into your life people who show you gently what you need to face until your mind softens enough to assimilate it. We need not be abrasive to each other, but only commit mutually to honoring evidence. We become change agents by saying to someone, "It seems to me that X is true but we're doing Y. Does it seem so to you?" We stand there, holding up the evidence of contradictory poles before them until they face it.

Fernando Flores, former Finance Minister of Chile and consultant to large companies, offered an insight into the need. He was summoned to the aid of an international corporation losing $100 million a year in a single division. Its crack management team had reduced losses to $10 million but was halted there and brought in Flores as their "last hope."

Sitting in on a meeting, he observed one manager with an attitude, another proposing something he personally did not believe in, another reacting with a superficial comment, and so on. He pointed out that *this competent management team accepted mediocre thinking.* He proposed instead that they challenge each other gracefully, thank each other for the comment, and promise further discussion about the issue.[5]

Emotional overtones make mediocre thinking slippery. Nearly every thought in need of correction is feeling based but perhaps not overtly. When rational evidence is consistently ignored, we justly suspect emotional reasons at play. Often such content simply narrows the scope of thinking, pruning away other ideas that could correct it. Pride, envy, and resentment can cloak themselves in apparent rationality as though the course selected were the only one conceivable. Our biggest problems usually follow from willfully misreading information there for the taking.

Several clues suggest that you check yourself for mediocre thinking:

1. You get poor results you didn't see coming.
2. You hear yourself discount others' thinking when they try to present a different perspective. Because you think you already *know,* you regard their thinking as superfluous.
3. You form your identity around unhelpful habits: "I'm assertive" even if your bluntness hurts others' feelings, or "I'm easy going" even if the job does not get done.
4. You rely on group think, connecting with others of similar belief while discounting contrary viewpoints.

5. You leap impulsively to premature conclusions, declaring what a small scrap of evidence means.
6. Your thinking reflects, unfiltered, the thoughts you pick up from random sources that align with your prejudices.
7. Your personal reference group may emphasize distorted thinking, like "Don't let anyone 'dis' you" or "Disagreement equals dislike."
8. Even though systems fail to work, you hold on to them because they operate with *your* ideas, and you like your ideas better than other people's—"which you're *supposed* to do, aren't you?" No. No, you are not.

THE DISCIPLINE OF CHANGE

You should prefer the *best* ideas and adopt them as fast as you can find them. Successful people distinguish themselves by not allowing irrationality to destroy what they create. They refuse to let their mood, a temporary feeling, a lazy assumption, a premature conclusion, or a divergent thought derail a constructive aim.

Preferring our own ideas over those of others makes us vulnerable to believing we're safer when others agree with us rather than when they challenge us, taking their agreement as confirming our correctness. Avoiding challenging feedback may cause actual damage, however. Others may reinforce our cognitive limitations, tolerate our idiosyncrasies, skirt our blind spots, or judge us too fragile to grasp a more substantial thought. They may edge around us "like walking on egg shells," and say to each other, "Don't bring that up around him or he'll just take off on it." You may avoid frank feedback because you know you would be uncomfortable.

This suggests a rule of thumb about what to look for in your direct experience: *Probe deeper into what makes you uncomfortable.* Located in that dark well are likely to be ideas you have avoided despite their value. By instead taking special interest in them, you narrow your search for ideas likely to be helpful. Practice recognizing the quality of your thinking and how it affects your life, and apply this to your work. Does your school system in issue after issue embody mediocre thinking, and if so, how does it impact your efforts?

When you avoid looking at ideas that make you uncomfortable, poorer ones inevitably run your life. Immersing yourself only in what agrees with you, you fail to notice pending injury.

Realities about human nature suggest eight guidelines:

1. *Change can be hard.* To expand even our capacity for change, we need to notice first how we resist it. Jim Rohn, an inspirational speaker, repeatedly explained to his audiences, "Tell me your past and I'll tell you your future." He could do that, he said, because *patterns continue.* People

think tomorrow as they thought yesterday, and change only within a narrow band.

An illustration. In the 1800s, naval cannons were extremely inaccurate. Warships could park at a distance from each other and fire all day without hitting anything. One day toward the close of the century, an officer on a British vessel doing practice firing noticed that a gunner made more hits than others by attempting continuous aim firing.

As the ship rolled back and forth with the cannon blasts, the seaman tried steadily to adjust its clumsy elevating mechanism. The officer quickly devised a more responsive one, improving aim dramatically, and an American ship adopting the changes obtained the same results.[6]

Pause here to consider an institution—the Navy or a school system. How would it respond? Rationally, one would expect that a simple change validated by evidence would quickly be applied everywhere, but it was not. *The Navy resisted the change so strenuously that President Theodore Roosevelt had to order it to be adopted.*

Social scientists investigating the resistance later came upon three main reasons. 1) Some people were just rebels. They did not want to do it just because you told them to. 2) Some were attached to their equipment, like a loyalty to "Old Betsy." 3) Others resisted changing the lifestyle around the use of existing equipment.

Check yourself by these reasons any of us might face: Do you sometimes fight a new idea *just because* someone else asks you to consider it? Do you find your familiar tools reassuring because you are accustomed to them? Have you woven a lifestyle around activities you do not want to upset?

To change your thinking substantially, you will need to loosen your claim on previous ideas more than you might expect. A woman commenting on changes in her life said, "Anything I ever let go of had *claw marks* all over it!" Adopting better ideas requires an exceptional willingness to be open, to learn, to listen, and to think outside our self-imposed box. We need to be constantly alert against interdicting our progress as old thinking resurges.

Our preset expectations can extend to teaching. We believe we have figured out some things by our years of experience, and other issues we leave alone as not ours. Upon encountering certain ideas in this book, you might think, "Well, I disagree with *that.*" Well you might. Angles pursued here are often ignored, and some could be wrong. But if what is written here is true, transformation of education is available for the taking.

2. *Change can occur quickly* even though hard, once the correct course of action is understood. When a group tilts, large numbers can move together in the same direction despite the difficulty with which individuals change. Recent history offers examples. Think how suddenly, startling the world, the Soviet Empire broke into constituent nations, how the

world's focus turned when Sputnik went into space, the changes that have occurred since 2001, and the startling uprisings in the Middle East. Events can catalyze the emotions of numbers of people who then express themselves through momentum for common action.

Social scientists tell us that current stability is no insurance for the future but is often instead a harbinger. Historian Arnold Toynbee explained that the best indicator that profound change was about to occur in a civilization was when everything seemed conquered, accomplished, and under control.[7]

Perhaps U.S. education hastening toward standardization is about to hurl itself in front of comprehensive change, although this may not occur easily because *rewards to current participants obstruct changes that redistribute rewards.* Those benefitting now carry an automatic bias against anything destabilizing and often must relinquish an advantage for the system to yield more benefits overall. Refusing to alter current rewards equals defense of the old system.

The accuracy of a new analysis becomes evident with a different effort/results ratio. As effort gets you nowhere and you finally understand what to do, your experience reverses. A *little* effort obtains *a lot* of results. On-target change is rapid. One doctor treats you fruitlessly for a year, and another gets it right the first visit and the problem is solved. In school, an interested child may still fail when his teacher does not understand how to guide his effort. Another offers clear steps and the student succeeds. Same child, different effort.

Student moods can shift rapidly as well. In one room, they are bored and distracted. They move down the hall to a different teacher and in minutes are focused and attentive. Same students but different conditions. The second teacher knew something the other did not. If we are frustrated with student behavior, we can assume that the conditions we arrange are ineffective and we need to do something else.

3. *Attitudes can change fast.* Every one of us possesses a range of moods. Some swing from hysterical to withdrawn in seconds while for most of us, steadier traits predominate. Children's moods, however, are exceptionally susceptible to immediate conditions. They are readily uplifted and engaged in one moment, and negative and contrary in another.

Two big influences affecting this shift are their perception of how their peer group treats them and the attitude of adults toward them. Influence from peers can aid countless changes. Peer tutoring, for instance, offers many known benefits. We can ask them to acknowledge how others give them good feelings, notice their own and others' use of communication skills, rate their experiences with each other in ways that assure them they are noticed, and affirm their success with peer applause. We can help them reinforce each other's better behaviors and feelings.

4. *Deep learning is possible.* While received wisdom is that "all children can learn," a nuance overlooked is that at a crucial stage *all learn the same*

way. Everyone has the same physiological structures—a brain system that perceives, encodes, and saves knowledge. In the saving portion, the standard steps could be described thus: "Grasp a chunk of knowledge, save it, grasp another, save both, grasp a third and integrate all three. Grasp another and add it to the group. Save everything." *Everyone does this to learn anything regardless of the perceptual doorway through which it entered.*

Some object to this picture on the basis that children need to estimate, reason, create, and weigh ideas, implicitly denying that they have to save learning consciously. While such processes are vital aspects of learning, *is it possible* to employ them without remembering them and the data they draw upon?

The question answers itself. You cannot use anything you cannot remember or cannot extrapolate from what you remember. Processes rely on steps children must install in mind. You double a child's flexibility about an issue by reminding him that he has two options instead of the one he was fixed on, but *he has to remember the second.*

Another misunderstanding about deep learning results from the different ways students may initially grasp knowledge. One teacher may assign reading (eye) while another gives an inspirational lecture (ear and emotion). One involves everyone in research (precise details), another in reporting (social reciprocity), and another does writing and experiments (kinesthetic). One assigns homework (planning and responsibility), and another relies on extended discussions (elaboration of ideas). Information arrives on the front porch of the brain from many directions, so bringing it that far is not our problem.

The problem is that *we have to change the means in order to sink the knowledge deeper.* We cannot just continue placing more information on the front porch of perception. When something reaches your front porch, the appropriate next step is to welcome it inside the house. Most instruction receives new knowledge only as a temporary guest. Do you not "finish" a section and then instruct students to drop it and go on?

Too many assume incorrectly that learning must inevitably evaporate and nothing can be done about it. Any functioning adult is evidence of the opposite. Each of us possesses a body of knowledge we use to survive, and all obtained it the same way. *We got a point, kept it, got another, and kept it.* However many we discarded, the ones we use are those we went back to, retrieved, and continued to apply.

Much instruction only salvages clues that *at one time* this student knew it, whether or not he still does. And even this moment of knowing may have occurred only after cramming, a guarantee of forgetting it quickly.

5. *Aligning instruction with students' innate tendencies* makes it easy. Human nature possesses many inborn inclinations that enable people to cope with the world. If we can, we piggyback instruction on them. We seldom expect to supply children an ability they lack completely but instead identify an existing capacity, such as focusing attention on a point

of knowledge, and help it grow along a channel that serves learning. We redirect what is already there.

Doing this sidesteps a struggle between adult demands and student inclinations. The latter are neutral, to be employed for good or ill. If inclined to follow group norms, students can find them in a drug-dealing ring or on a school wrestling team. Aligning a student tendency with our instructional purpose, our effort becomes more effective.

The Theory of Minimum Change applies here. If we have two ways to achieve an outcome, one costing us three and the other seven units of effort, we choose the three so we can use the remaining four for something else. The three option represents the easy way, yet set in our ways we can still require the seven or even misguidedly commit to one costing us thirteen. To be efficient with our time and avoid struggle with students, we choose what accomplishes the goal elegantly by drawing on existing tendencies. Here are a few with a possible application of each:

- Desire to "make it" in their peer group → "Make it" by constructive communications and relationships
- Desire for clear instructions → Clear instructions about how to learn
- Talk to friends → Talk to friends about learning
- Show off → Show off about learning
- Develop competences → Develop competences by learning
- Feel good → Feel good about making others feel good
- Feel good → Feel good about learning
- Relax → Increase inner balance and concentration
- Listen → Enable someone else to develop their ideas
- Desire for self-affirmation → Learn how to manage emotions
- Play → Play with the content of learning
- Create → Create with the content of learning

We can arrange for nearly any classroom activity to draw on a natural tendency.

6. *Perceive accurately the reality you can respond to constructively.* Knowing what we are doing is harder to pull off than it may appear. When we find our efforts going wrong or not yielding expected results, we can presume that our picture is faulty. We may not even realize that we unwittingly reinforce the wrong thing. Unconscious patterning can hinder us from noticing that we have a choice about which of several aspects to focus on.

Perceiving what we expect is the first problem. Many teachers do not actually see what they look at but rather see what their mind braces them against. Observing a child with an attitude, their temptation is to remount their own attitude rather than notice, say, a nine-year-old struggling to understand feelings in turmoil and unsteady outer circumstances. The reality we select to respond to can make all the difference.

In a second grade class, two students are not nice to each other. The counselor stands them facing each other and asks, "What can you respect or admire in each other?"

At first the girl cannot think of anything, but finally says, "He's good at football."

"Okay, from now on," the counselor says, "whenever you think of him, I want you to think just about him being good at football. Can you do that?" She nods.

Then the counselor turns to the boy and asks what he knows about her that he can respect. After a long pause, he says, "In first grade, we used to be friends." She smiles.

"Okay now," the counselor says to him, "whenever you think of her, just remember that in first grade you used to be friends. Can you do that?" He nods.

"Can you shake hands on that?" the counselor asks. They grin at each other and shake hands.

This may not have solved their problem entirely, but the principle is clear. If you *choose* to cast this person negatively, you have no hope for even a constructive—to say nothing of friendly—relationship.

A girl struggles to unlearn a deep-seated conviction that the world is against her. She is trying to change while her teacher has dismissed her as a manipulator. Questionable behaviors are indeed woven into her approach to life, but laying such an accusation upon her can never help her change. Looking at her, one must notice a different truth, like a young person who realizes she is not happy and would genuinely like to be different.

A second problem is that limitations can arise in what appears at first to be an unqualified positive. It has been said, for instance, that "a principal must want something for his/her school." Leaders give emotional meaning to the effort they ask of others so that it infuses what they do.

Teachers apply this to students, *wanting* this one to find self-respect, that one to experience a sense of completion, another to discover acceptance and good feelings with peers, and another to take pride in a job well done. One can want a perfect school to emerge from everyone's efforts.

But wanting has a con side. It can appear to others as an invasion, an attempt to control them, or a demand for a step they are not ready to take. People do not like *our* wanting for them to replace their own. Wanting stretches beyond the present reality and commits our energy against an obstacle. We want what we perceive we do not have, assigning our energy to the sense of lack, and may compound a problem by misreading reality. We may want something not accessible, a bridge too far, so that our wanting creates needless distress based on a mistake.

What do we do? Do we stop wanting, promote what we want, or surrender to what others want? A largely forgotten virtue is *balance,* an internal state freed from being pulled every which way. Balance enables the mind to release its preconceptions, and in their place accept *what arrives as actuality.*

We want to notice it when information tells us what is truly available from appropriate effort. We want to recognize the potential in the situation and match our effort to its conditions, to notice what students intrinsically want and align with it, stretching outside the self-interested, ego-driven needs that may color our self-image. Our hearts expand to want the best for all. We shift from narrow to broad thinking and notice the good available to all concerned if we unfix our viewpoint.

As we are ready to understand differently, we increase our organizational versatility. Although our personality may have its patterns, we can direct our mind to be open to the novel. *Any habitual emphasis excludes the benefits from everything we fail to notice.* Mounting our charger, we cease to attune ourselves to others, their feelings, their needs, the tentative ideas on the edge of their awareness, or questions they repress right when they could bring them up.

By inserting our personal mood into every situation, we cause it to override the delicate beginnings of self-expression in others. What if on the edge of a teacher's mind is a suggestion that, while incomplete, could solve a problem for the school? For such tentative thinking to be expressed, it awaits listening, respect, patience, and clarification from others. At a problem-solving session at a facility, the director of it talked the entire time until the meeting was over. A participant penned the following question on a piece of paper left on the table as everyone departed: "If I had a good idea, how would you elicit it from me?"

Tentative ideas are not developed in organizations required at every turn to carry out the top person's thought—an assessment that might apply to many schools organized top-down. That teachers in such an organization "don't have any ideas to offer" is an outcome of the structure. If leaders feel they waste time by creating conditions of listening and respect, others feel subdued and discounted, yet balance is always essential. Overuse of democratic decision making can slow an organization. Well-integrated groups often work better when a decisive leader takes speedy responsibility and relieves individuals of having to discuss everything.

The organization's interest extends beyond making people feel good, of course. The key instead is that *everybody thinks better than anybody* even if it takes some sparks to elicit all the salient ideas. Even an organization's best thinkers improve their results if they can incorporate the best ideas of everyone.

When we listen patiently, respect others, and clarify ideas, we may realize, "What you want to do is fine, but wait five minutes," or "This person has significant needs right now, so drop what you were about to do and pay attention to her," or "This minimal step was for this student an exhausting effort, so slow down and give her the recognition that helps her assimilate her action," or "This teacher needs to know we value her attempt to help," or finally, "This idea fits perfectly, just what we've been looking for."

Though we carry a general plan for the day, we are also ready to suspend our intentions in order to attend to new information. Remaining alert, our mind rises to the occasion to incorporate incoming perceptions, interpretations, and actions. We do not allow ourselves be saturated only by habitual thoughts and feelings.

7. *Ask yourself questions.* To know what you are doing, *you need to commit to a life of the mind,* using it to negotiate the path ahead that just may now be invisible, opening to you only a moment at a time. To prepare you for this journey, your mind needs to continually reflect on its circumstances and imagine how to handle them. You might select one idea per day to ponder until you know your next step with it:

- Students' need for mastered rather than familiarized knowledge.
- Students' need for personal responsibility.
- Students' need to handle feelings.
- How to tell whether an instruction or intervention fits those it is intended for.
- How to guide students' attention.
- How to bring out the best idea.
- Why constructing a mental field is important.
- How to construct a mental field.
- Why students need to talk about their own ideas.
- How to piggyback instruction on students' innate tendencies.
- How to change techniques so students work harder than the teacher does.
- Trading useful ideas for teaching.
- The means and importance of validating students.
- How to work with closed people.
- How personal traits affect success at implementing new strategies.
- How others may diminish one's motivation or ability to teach.
- How we let that happen or change it.
- What is required for transfer of training back to the classroom.
- What is needed to make a new idea usable.
- How a beginner's mind figures into learning new material.
- The conditions for retaining knowledge.
- What enhances children's ability to manage their emotions.
- How to become first cause of the learning in one's classroom.
- How mediocre thinking can limit our identity and actions.
- Habits of thought that work against us and how to change them.
- How we avoid feedback and how to reverse that.
- How to sustain and draw from the social milieu.

8. *Try being unusually receptive.* Open yourself to the novel angle as fully as you can. Maybe you will not end up discarding familiar ideas, but at least let in new ones long enough to weigh them. Think how you might have dodged the good ideas of competent people. Think through how you choose people to interact with, the kind of criticism or response you expect, and the role you play. Be able to say these things to people you trust:

- Do you have any feedback for me?
- What is your viewpoint about this?
- What is it like to work with me?
- How is it to be in a relationship with me?
- Please tell me something you think I should know.
- Can you suggest a way I could improve?
- Thanks for the heads up.
- I appreciate anything that keeps me out of trouble.
- Good idea. I'll think about that.
- Let me write it down so I can think about it later.
- Thank you for telling me that.
- Maybe we can talk more about it later.

Practice being at ease welcoming feedback. In the workplace with co-workers and supervisors, check your guesses about others' meaning and invite them to elaborate in detail. Admit mistakes rapidly and completely: "I got that wrong. I'm sorry. I'll try to make sure it doesn't happen again."

As you sort things out, remember the hang glider. It could have been built hundreds of years ago from common materials. So also with education. Familiar materials have been around nearly forever, but put together in a different way, they can offer longer flight time. Learn, save, learn, save, learn, save.

SUMMARY

1. Change can be hard because patterns continue.
2. Change can occur quickly once the correct course is understood.
3. The quality of thinking in schools tends to mirror the quality of thinking in society.
4. Rewards to current participants obstruct changes that would redistribute rewards.
5. We must keep students' effort on target.
6. Deep learning is possible by essentially the same methods for everyone.
7. After knowledge arrives in our perceptions, we must change our methods to sink it deeper.

8. Aligning instruction with students' innate tendencies makes it easier.
9. Perceive accurately the reality you can respond to constructively.
10. Any habitual emphasis excludes the benefits from everything we fail to notice.
11. Everybody thinks better than anybody, but this may generate sparks.
12. Prefer the best ideas over your own ideas.
13. A beginner's mind relinquishes an old idea to adopt a better one.
14. Ask yourself questions. Commit to a life of the mind.
15. Practice being at ease welcoming feedback. Peer deeper into what makes you uncomfortable.
16. Investing in mediocre thinking is the main reason for failure.

NOTES

1. A thoughtful reader may notice that this tack appears to contradict our earlier insistence that we focus on what we want rather than what we do not want. At an earlier position on the time track, however, is acknowledging the reality of the situation. Once facing it, we have a better chance of recognizing what might work.

2. Royce Van Norman, "School Administration: Thoughts on Organization and Purpose," *Phi Delta Kappan*, 47(1966): 315–316.

3. The consultant's name is Rick Schefren.

4. Michael J. O'Neill, "What We Want Depends on the Question," *Arizona Republic*, B12, January 4, 2009.

5. Harriet Rubin, "The Power of Words," *Fast Company*, December 31, 1998.

6. Warren G. Bennis, Kenneth D. Benne, and Robert Chin, *The Planning of Change: Readings in the Applied Behavioral Sciences* (New York: Holt, Rinehart and Winston, 1966) and Elting E. Morrison, "A Case Study of Innovation," *Engineering and Science*, 13(7), pp. 5-11, 1950

7. Arnold Toynbee with D. C. Somervell, *A Study of History: Abridgement of Vols. I–X in One Volume* (New York: Oxford University Press, 1960). Toynbee's major life work was the examination of the rise and fall of civilizations, supplying a detail-rich backdrop against which to recognize the progress of our own through rather typical stages. Such reading in schools, unknown in the first twelve years, could be a helpful antidote to the hubris often present as a country tries to assert an unreasonable intent.

TWELVE

Hold Out for the Plus Element

Even good education is not enough

We can assume that you are a good teacher. From wherever they start, in a year your students advance a year's progress or more. That you read a book like this is a positive sign. We can assume even that you absorb others' ideas to improve your outcomes.

Despite your efforts, the social system is in deep trouble. Problems outstrip solutions. Disaster could find us from several directions, threatening a fabric of society more fragile than most are willing to consider. Failing to recognize untamed forces is almost a guarantee that they will impale us at some point.

THREE FORCES NOT DEALT WITH

Despite the respected efforts of you and your colleagues, *the manner in which you probably teach now portends egregious problems for society*. For issues facing billions of people, the *common* manner of education fails to develop the quality of thought needed to address them.

Three reasons stand out. First, typical education does not enable children to counteract endemic forces of *collective irrationality*. Second, it does not teach them to manage *collective emotion*. Third, schools' preoccupation with children's individual competence at narrowly defined skills offers only the mere prologue to the *systemic problems* confronting society.

A group of high school girls argues loudly with a group of boys over why they do not get along. Each blames the other. Neither is interested in the other's viewpoint, in careful listening, nor in problem solving. None grasps that his or her own behavior causes the problem. They only want

161

to know who is to blame, dramatizing two destructive forces playing out in society: *irrationality driven by unmanaged emotion.*

We often see individuals become indignant for little cause over this or that, have opinions that wander far from the facts, and fail to reconcile contradictions in their thinking. Because they survive in society and even become its leaders and opinion setters, their limitations are installed in the social landscape. Some sort mailing addresses of the "emotional irrationals" into cohorts they can manipulate with micromarketing code words. Depth of thought and the resolution of competing ideas are dismissed so that people can be manipulated.

That this invites disaster is evident just within the last decade—the near-implosion of the financial system, our involvement in two wars, the growing unaddressed impact of global warming, the steady extinction of ocean life, and the depletion of natural resources.

Yet because anyone can find someone else who agrees, mainstream thought is left to evolve by the chance of mutually neutralizing contentions. Teachers K–12, often pressed to remain aloof from knotty issues of society's long-term well-being, must pay attention instead to whether students comply with guidelines enough for credits and graduation.

MEDIOCRE THINKING ABOUT PRINCIPLES

A system that welcomes such mediocre thinking into its core may face disaster even during stable eras that do not tax the intelligence, but those are long gone. Now unfamiliar choices erupt. Nations and individuals are transfixed by black swan situations, and more are certainly on the way. We are collectively unprepared to think about issues we have not already experienced.

But so what? We take comfort that civilization has survived and easily become complacent that prosperity is permanent. At many moments in the past, however, the educated responses needed were missing and we would like to know *what kind of education could have supplied them.*

Consider the Germans, among the most educated in the world early in the prior century, with many of the world's leading thinkers and innovators among them. How could they invent Nazism and inaugurate World War II and the Holocaust? How? Learning as it was usually thought of was not enough. Missing were the rule of law, respect for the individual, and tolerance of differences.

How could "the best and brightest" American leaders in the 1960s be drawn into a war in Vietnam that near-universal judgment now regards as unnecessary? How? They received the finest education available to Americans, yet it was irrelevant to their central judgments and may instead have exaggerated their confidence. Missing were a commitment to truth, reasoning based on evidence, facing one's opponents, and separating ideology from reality.

How could the United States have been drawn into an unneeded war in Iraq while ignoring unfinished business in Afghanistan after the events of 9/11? We were led by an anti-intellectual president who claimed to rely on his instincts. Americans superficially acquainted with the Middle East had not learned to weigh values, risk, and benefit with refined comprehension, and nothing in their education stood in their way. Missing were a respect for knowledge, restraint on the use of coercive power, and respect for the autonomy of other nations.

How could leaders a half century ago ignore compelling scientific evidence even then that human activity was warming the globe and that disaster could ensue unless easy steps were taken then that are impossible now? Scientists explained the trends to Congress, but those responsible for the nation refused to project causality into the future. Missing were a sense of cause and effect, a long-range view, and present responsibility for the future.

Cast your eye further back. How could an educated, religious people for almost three centuries in the New World continue to justify slavery? One can blame cultural expectations, which begs the question of the role of education. If excesses exist and are tolerated, should education help free us from them? If it does not, if we cannot count on our collective best judgment to check our worst, then survival is just by luck. Missing were a perception of common humanity, skepticism of self-serving rationalization, and a humanitarian spirit.

Recent threats to the economy arose as the seeking for personal gain undermined the best interest of the whole, a concern deliberately dismissed by leaders. Schooling as we know it does not instruct students how to think with balance, objectivity, and responsibility for the whole but prefers idiosyncrasy instead. "Do your own thing" justifies selfishness, and "Live and let live" disclaims responsibility for others' destructiveness. Missing were altruism balancing greed, truth displacing deception, and the common good balancing individual gain.

Far-sighted people long ago tried to safeguard our government through a balance of powers between legislative, executive, and judicial branches. The fragility of the balance was demonstrated when, upon the excuse of 9/11, the long-standing prohibition of torture was shredded by government leaders. They defended the necessity of torture, imprisonment without charges, and suspension of the right to a trial, and repeatedly ignored privacy rights. Missing were the practical implications of individual rights and the rule of law.

Examples can be extended, but we might tally up what's missing so far in the thinking that has led to disasters:

1. Rule of law

2. Respect for the individual
3. Tolerance of differences
4. Altruism balancing greed
5. Truth displacing deception
6. Common good balancing individual gain
7. Perception of common humanity
8. Questioning self-serving rationalization
9. A humanitarian spirit
10. An appreciation of cause and effect
11. A long-term view
12. Present responsibility for the future
13. A respect for knowledge
14. Restraint on the use of coercive power
15. Respect for the autonomy of other nations
16. Facing one's opponents
17. Balancing ideology with empirical evidence

That these elements are largely absent from education today might alarm us, but even worse is that *good teachers failed to address them.* They were hired to do a job and did it. They transmitted society's accommodations but not its ideals.

We need to grasp the overall picture. The events listed above were irrational, often morally destructive, and driven by unmanaged emotion, yet public opinion supported them. We can infer that the population as a whole did not obtain from education the competence to think them through.

They could not examine the tradeoffs of values in a refined way, nor separate emotion from the interpretation of evidence, nor prevent personal motives from warping reasoning. They ignored the conflict between behavior and values, and allowed ideology to displace both values and grounded rationality.

SUCCEED AND CREATE BIGGER PROBLEMS

If this is true, it suggests that current attempts to reform American schools are likely to be inadequate *even if they reach their objectives.* We do not solve the problems above just with better teachers because those who led us into those problems *succeeded* in their education. Their teachers were good to excellent, and therefore hiring and training such teachers will not prevent such problems.

To design education in light of this picture, we face a more exacting standard, like the difference between running laps and doing brain surgery. *We seek balanced emotional self-management linked with a sensitive and accurate picture of the world to produce judgment pruned of distortion.* Hold that criterion in mind as you re-invent education because that is where you need to end up.

Students do not reliably obtain such thinking anywhere else. Church and family are everywhere, exerting what influence they can. Not only could they not avert the disasters above but sometimes led the way into them, leaving the question open, "Who will generate the thinking that can meet the challenges of the future?" Only society itself can take responsibility for the activities that define it.

We do not meet these needs just by adding a new course to the curriculum. Our problem is more substantial than disagreements over information or politics. It rests in a zone of personal consciousness that education usually addresses only peripherally, but its impact on society's survival bids us tackle it. Truly successful schools affect this zone deeply. They teach their graduates how to manage themselves to produce a constructive life.

It is no stretch to imagine society dividing in half.[1] People on one side learn everything needed for a civilized society, while those on the other replace learning with slogans and labels. Only the former can resolve civilization's problems. Those who think humbly and deliberately, and who know how hard rational thought can be, have at least a hope of producing solutions. To obtain such mastery, one must intend it and commit to the effort required.

THE EFFORT IS UP TO YOU

Student effort. *Satisfying* student effort. Right now, with your available resources, you can steer it toward mastery if you want. Doing so depends, I believe, on a rather small shift in your thinking.

Imagine that for a handsome salary, you were hired to tutor the son of a dictator in a remote country. You become acquainted with the lad and other palace children in your charge. After a few days, the dictator summons you to his office, leans back behind a desk the size of a football field, and his face darkens. He slaps the desk with a huge hand and declares about his son, *"I want him to learn something!"*

You return to your comfortable quarters pondering this. What could he mean? Is he implying that as you stroll about the palace grounds chatting with the lad and his friends, that the boy is not learning something? Or that the movies you watch together, or the field trips you lead, or the many papers you process are not educational? The import of an answer rises as you discover from the cook that the dictator was unhappy with the last person to occupy your post and he disappeared abruptly.

You decide to interpret the dictator's words conservatively. *You make sure your young charge can answer any question his father could ask about what he learns.* In whatever you instruct the children, you make sure they have absorbed its meaning, can tell it back, and discuss what they share. You prepare your student to meet his father in the evening and say happily, *"Daddy, let me tell you everything I learned today!"*

As you followed the story, note that you supplied the child's age, subjects, resources, motivation to learn, cooperativeness, and number of fellow students—left out to make a point: *They are not determinative.* The same standard holds whether the child is kindergarten or high school, the subjects standard or off-beat, resources plentiful or few, the child cooperative or uncooperative, the class large or small. Regardless of the variance in conditions, we certify that this child "learns something" as he can deliberately call it up and maintain it at that level—continuous conscious mastery.

You apply such a standard only as it is important to you. Maybe working for a salary does not move you and students' needs might not either, but your life depending on it might. You would go after unarguable evidence of it. You would discard teaching practices that gave only lip service to results; you would choose mastery instead of familiarization, explaining a subject in depth instead of relying on clues and hints.

You would insist that everyone got the whole answer, not just some just partly, and would skewer the lazy dodges behind much of what we accept for children. Who could be against the paper and pencil exercises, arts and crafts to illustrate ideas, hand-made posters on the wall, and good experiences that immerse them in familiar perceptions?

Children are too hurried anyway, are they not? And they need "hands-on," do they not? And we do not want to stress them, do we? And they cannot take home everything they learn anyway, can they? And companionship with us means learning is occurring does it not? With a skeptical dictator peering at us, we refuse to allow half-truths to distract us but go after real learning.

Do not accept mediocre outcomes when you can get mastery. You have powerful tools at hand: students' tendencies you can enlist, their interest in what peers think of them, their delight in good leadership, hours of effort you can channel, and valid mastery to aim for.

And once confident you can teach them anything they need to know, turn their attention to the plus element—how the exercise of their mind may help civilization survive.

SUMMARY

1. The manner in which you probably teach portends egregious problems for society.
2. Educated responses that could have forestalled big problems of the past were missing.

3. We want to know what kind of education could have supplied them.
4. Education has overlooked the rule of law, respect for the individual, tolerance of differences, altruism balancing greed, truth displacing deception, common good balancing individual gain, perception of common humanity, questioning self-serving rationalization, a humanitarian spirit, an appreciation of cause and effect, a long-term view, present responsibility for the future, a respect for knowledge, restraint on the use of coercive power, respect for the autonomy of other nations, facing one's opponents, and balancing ideology with empirical evidence.
5. We seek balanced emotional self-management linked with a sensitive and accurate picture of the world to produce judgment pruned of distortion.
6. Do not accept mediocre outcomes when you can get mastery.

NOTE

1. Charles Murray, *Coming Apart: The State of White America 1960–2010* (New York: Random House, 2012). Murray presents an alarming picture of the differences and separateness between smart/elite and poor/ignorant sectors of white society. While his analysis of the causes behind it is incomplete, he documents its features extensively.